The Mystic's Way
for Regular People

The Mystic's Way
for Regular People

JAMES C. ALEXANDER

RESOURCE *Publications* · Eugene, Oregon

THE MYSTIC'S WAY FOR REGULAR PEOPLE

Resource Publications
An Imprint of Wipf and Stock Publishers
199 W. 8th Ave., Suite 3
Eugene, OR 97401

www.wipfandstock.com

PAPERBACK ISBN: 978-1-7252-9341-0
HARDCOVER ISBN: 978-1-7252-9342-7
EBOOK ISBN: 978-1-7252-9343-4

03/23/21

For Bishop Bill Smalley who is
(as my friend Diane says) the real deal.
And for Pat Connell,
my fellow brother and pilgrim on the way.

Contents

Acknowledgments

SPECIAL THANKS TO ALL the folks that read the manuscript and commented on it. Your comments led to changes for the better. Special thanks to Fr. Pat Connell. This isn't the first time he has served as a reader for me. His comments are always insightful. Diane Burrell read the manuscript and offered many useful comments. Thanks to Gabe Sinisi from my Poverello Fellowship group for a quick turn around on reading the manuscript and for sharing his thoughts. Hawley Todd from Sister Water Fellowship gave me a great deal to think about regarding the book. My son, Aaron, and my daughter-in-law, Maria, helped with the initial editing. Aaron helped a great deal with some computer stuff I just "don't get." (It helps to have a software engineer son!) My sister, Elsetta Torres, read several chapters while they were still in embryonic format and offered her encouragement. Father Matt and Cate Zimmermann, two very dear, longtime friends read several chapters. Debbie Wepler provided most helpful editing expertise. My son, Galen, and his wife, Purvi Patel, live a long way off. But, I must say that their calls helped me get my mind off of this project from time to time, for which I am grateful; I am glad they are in my life. Finally, special thanks to my wife, Irene. I never consider writing much of anything, without her input.

Introduction

Guard against all pride, vanity, envy, avarice, the cares and
worries of this world, detraction, and complaining. And if you
do not have book-learning, do not be eager to acquire it, but
pursue instead what you should desire above all else, namely,
to have the Spirit of the Lord and his grace working in you, to
pray always with purity of heart and to have humility, patience
in persecution and in infirmity, and to love those who persecute
and rebuke and slander you, because the Lord says, "Love your
enemies and pray for those who persecute you." (Mt. 5:44)

—St. Francis

Somehow, I think that St. Francis really gets to the heart of the
gospel, the good news. Christianity is not really about learned theology or being so consumed with self that we lose focus on others.
It is really about God's grace operating in our hearts, and praying—talking with God, listening to God—with a pure heart. All of
this should lead to a new life. It should guide the way for us to be
new creations in Christ, living with Kingdom values, indeed living
life on a whole new basis (2 Corinthians 5:17).

I read this quote from Francis recently in the context of the
Daily Office (Morning Prayer), which I pray every day as part of
my vow of obedience as a Third Order Franciscan (TSSF). I have
read similar thoughts expressed by the saints and church fathers

and mothers many times over the years. My question has always been "How?" How do I live a life not centered on self? How do I let go of the worries of the world? How do I live a life filled with love and joy? To all this St. Francis and that Great Cloud of Witnesses would answer, "Get to know Jesus."

After many years of college teaching, I think I am qualified to say that young people will always have a youth culture with which they identify. I was a child of the 60's and 70s. As a teenager, I was drawn to the youth subculture of my day—something my parents, especially my dad, just didn't understand. But, in the midst of all of change that characterized those times, something happened that forever changed my life. Young people were stirring with a thirst for some spiritual truth; something that was real; something that would last. I too was a searcher. And my search led me to the Jesus People. These folks were mostly former society dropouts and those who, like me, were attracted to the current hippie subculture.

Love won out, and I found myself praying to be "born again." My outlook was wholly Evangelical. It seemed that at last, I had found Jesus. I began to tell my friends and family, "Try Jesus, he's real." For quite a while, I seemed happy and fulfilled.

But, deep within, something was missing. The Jesus People talked a great deal about knowing Jesus as your personal savior. Still, even though I prayed about it constantly, I didn't really feel that I knew God. It was all a matter of faith, or so I was told. And I did believe. I believed that Jesus had saved me from my emptiness; that he had saved me from hell. But, no matter what, my faith just didn't seem to be enough.

To make a long story short, my search for something more led me to go to seminary where I worked on a graduate degree with an emphasis in church history. I began my studies at an American Baptist seminary until my wife and I needed to relocate. I ended up graduating from a Roman Catholic seminary with a degree in historical theology. Through all of this I encountered the writings of the church Mothers and Fathers and the saints who seemed to always be talking about knowing God in a real way.

Introduction

For the Fathers and Mothers of the faith, faith was real, and it drove them to their knees. Knowing God was not primarily about being saved or escaping hell. It wasn't about fire insurance. Knowing God was about a face-to-face communion with God—a participation in the very life of God. It was about a love affair. This was very different than what I had learned from the Jesus People (though, I must admit, they likely saved my life).

After this followed several years of ministry as a minister in a small Presbyterian denomination and twenty-five years of work as a college professor. Over those years, I have discovered that most folks seem to have something missing in their lives; a hole in the heart. They try to fill that empty space with many things. Yet, in some measure, they always seem to still have that emptiness.

I don't have any easy answers to all of this, but I do have my own experience. I can share some of where I've been going theologically, and that matters. But, even more important, I can share where I am going spiritually. If you are someone searching for something more; I am writing this book for you. If you have been on the road for a long time and have discovered that your old familiar way of making the journey just isn't working, this book is for you. If you are seeking an encounter with love, this book is for you. This little book on mysticism is offered as an answer to the loneliness and existential emptiness that we all feel.

1

What is Mysticism?

IF WE WERE TO consult a dictionary or encyclopedia to discover what mysticism is, we would find general agreement. Mysticism is the art of union with the ultimate. It can refer to direct union with God or, in the case of non-theistic mystics, a union with the universe. In general, the union is non-dualistic. By this we mean that the walls are removed when we are united with reality, and we experience ourselves as part of the whole. However, in Christian mysticism, the mystic does not become God. But, he or she does share in the divine nature. As 2 Peter 1:4 states, we become *"partakers of the divine nature."*

The Eastern Church has always held to the idea that we can share in the nature of God. St. Athanasius put it clearly, "The Son of God became man that we might become God." This may sound radical, but it has a long history in Christian thought. For the church Fathers and Mothers, this did not mean that humans became what God is- Creator, Redeemer, and Sanctifier. It means that, by grace, we become what Jesus is by nature.

At its heart, mysticism is a radical identification with ultimate reality. It is communion with that reality, which for Christians is the reality of God. In mysticism, seekers seek to have a direct experience of God. Traditionally, it has been thought that certain practices would assist seekers in their journey to a direct experience of God. For example, monastics typically live under a set of rules that are designed to lead to union with God. Many folks associate mysticism with "woo-woo" or some sort of esoteric New Age philosophy. This is partially because of claims by mystics that they have "found God." It is also because many of the traditional practices used by mystics in the search for God seem unusual or odd in the eyes of everyday folks.

Mystics very often seek solitude. They take literally Jesus' words telling his followers to pray in secret: *"But whenever you pray, go into your room and shut the door and pray to your Father who is in secret; and your Father who sees in secret will reward you,"* (Matthew 6:6). Mystics often utilize methods developed over the centuries to focus the heart on God and quiet the mind so that they can better hear. These practices include Lectio Divina, Centering Prayer, meditation, and use of prayer beads or ropes. Many Christian mystics take time to focus on and pray the Jesus Prayer ("Jesus, Son of God, have mercy on me, a sinner.").

In general, the Christians mystics have discerned a progression of growth in the knowledge of God. Although some mystics, such as Theresa of Avila and John of the Cross described several sequential stages from beginner to a state of union with God, earlier writers generally described three stages: repentance, contemplation, and union. In the first stage, the seeker of God turns from their sins and seeks healing of their essential brokenness. In the second stage, the seeker meditates upon the nature of God and God's dealings in their heart and life. This stage involves effort from the seeker, as does repentance. All of this leads to the third stage—union with God. This union is a fruit of repentance and contemplation and is a gift of God.

Alfred North Whitehead, whom we will encounter in the next chapter, sees knowledge acquisition as a cyclical process. There is a stage of romance that is exploratory and excited, almost playful. The next stage is a stage of deepening understanding and involvement with the object of our attention. The final stage is one of full comprehension. Or so it seems. However, Whitehead says that there is always more to experience, so when we reach the highest stages, we ultimately find ourselves as beginners once more. So, it seems to be with our spiritual journey. We begin and progress in our relationship with God. But, just when it seems that we have arrived, we realize that we have not arrived after all, and so we must start a new romance with God once again.

Sometimes, mystics have had extrasensory experiences and visions. Some, like Pascal, have experienced trancelike states, ecstatic visions of dazzling light- the apostle Paul seems to have experienced this as well, (see 2 Corinthians 12:1–10). Peter uses the word "trance" to describe his visionary experience (see Acts 11:4–10)]. Sometimes they appear to be carried away in a joyful reverie. Yet Christian mystics such as John of the Cross advise against seeking supernatural experiences and even caution that such an experience can be a distraction from the main goal of communion with God in Christ.

Every religious tradition seems to have mystical overtones. This is true of South Asian religions, Islam, Judaism, and Christianity. It seems that a mystic response to the ultimate reality is a common thing for all people. In fact, surveys have shown that at least one-third of Americans claim to have had some type of mystical experience. These were experiences where the individual is overcome by a sense of love or wonder at the beauty of nature, or caught up in the quiet of the moment. In his wonderful book, *The Roots of Christian Mysticism*, Olivier Clément explores a great many patristic (from the earliest years of the church) texts and demonstrates that a mystical understanding of the Christian faith was common, maybe even the *most common* understanding of what being a Christian was all about in the patristic era. Psychologists speak of a state known as "flow," where time is unnoticed and we seem to be absorbed in the moment or activity in which we are engaged. In the classic writings about religion and religious experiences, William James spoke about mystical moments that are perceived as beyond day-to-day consciousness. Such experience may not only be found in religious contexts, but also in secular contexts. Human psychology seems to have equipped us with the ability to have mystical encounters with reality.

Christian mysticism is different, in that in Christian approaches utilize our common human tendency for mystical experience, but then turn it toward God in Christ. We are focusing our attention on a search for God. We know that we have the ability to have experiences outside of normal consciousness. In a Christian approach, we attempt to quiet our arguments, hassles, concerns, and worries about the world and our lives. Once quieted, we focus our attention on God and knowing God.

In *The Big Book of Christian Mysticism*, Carl McColeman describes Christian mysticism as Christianity's "best kept secret." It is ancient and not some "program" cooked up by someone in the recent past. Its roots are in the New Testament. It is not like ordinary religious experience. Mysticism is closely tied to mystery and subjective experience. At its base, it is about fully loving God, and by loving God, fully loving others.

Rufus Jones was a Quaker mystic who completed his masterful *Studies in Mystical Religion* in 1909. He was careful in the use of the term mysticism because it can be off putting and hard to define. He was concerned about the esoteric connotations that the word evoked. Therefore, he was careful to use the word to express a certain type of religious experience that emphasizes a direct consciousness of God's presence and an "immediate awareness of relation with God." Jones felt that this was "religion in its most acute, intense and living stage."

MYSTICISM IN SCRIPTURE

There is a long tradition of mysticism in the Jewish and Christian traditions. In modern times this is still apparent in the surge of interest in Jewish Kabbalah and the Christian practice of Centering Prayer. It is also apparent in virtually all religious traditions. In Islam, we see the dominance of mystical thinking in Sufism. Buddhism has a very strong element of non-theistic mysticism. Many mystical practices such as meditation and Yoga have roots deeply planted in the religions of India.

In Judeo-Christian tradition(s), the mystic idea is widely represented in the Hebrew scriptures (the Old Testament) and in the New Testament. We cannot even begin, in this brief book, to look at all of the texts which speak of folks having a direct experience of God and even supernatural experiences usually termed mystical. It will be instructive, however, to look at a few passages to get a taste of the mystical nature of the Bible. So . . . here we go . . .

Luke 5:16—But Jesus would withdraw to deserted places and pray.

In this passage, we see Jesus engaging in a practice that seems to be a regular feature of his life. Jesus spent his days among the people, healing the sick and preaching Good News to the poor. Christians believe that Jesus is the unique incarnation of God, and their model and example for faith and action. Even though Jesus was quite intentional in his active life, and was definitely a man with a mission, he still spent time in quiet talking with God.

Hosea 2:20—I will take you for my wife in faithfulness; and you shall know the Lord.

In this passage, the prophet likens the relationship between God and God's people to the relationship between marriage partners. Just as such partners know each other better than anyone else knows either of them, so God wants to know God's people and for God's people to know God.

Hosea 6:3—Let us know, let us press on to know the Lord . . .

Once again, Hosea speaks about knowing God. Here, the prophet encourages God's people to "press on" to know God. Religion is not just about (or even mostly about) keeping rules and fulfilling required rituals and requirements. It is about knowing God. Loving God with all of our heart, soul, and mind.

First Kings 19:11–13—He said, "Go out and stand on the mountain before the Lord, for the Lord is about to pass by." Now there was a great wind, so strong that it was splitting mountains and breaking rocks in pieces before the Lord, but the Lord was not in the wind; and after the wind an earthquake, but the Lord was not in the earthquake; and after the earthquake a fire, but the Lord was not in the fire; and after the fire a sound of sheer silence. When Elijah heard it, he wrapped his face in his mantle and went out and stood at the entrance of the cave.

Elijah, in this story, is depressed, afraid, lonely, and discouraged. He needs to encounter God that he might find his center once again. God does meet with Elijah. But, God doesn't come in miraculous events and with breathtaking signs. God comes to Elijah in the silence. This story reminds us that God is most often found in the quiet and in the act of listening more than speaking.

Revelation 3:20—Listen! I am standing at the door, knocking; if you hear my voice and open the door, I will come in to you and eat with you, and you with me.

Here, Jesus is saying that he is waiting outside the door of our hearts wanting to gain entrance. In the world of John the Revelator, dining with someone meant much more than just sharing food. It spoke of friendship, honoring, caring and welcoming. Jesus wants to know us, to have dinner with us. There is however one requirement. We must listen and hear his voice.

Luke 17:21—The kingdom of God is among you.

This passage may be saying more than one thing. The NRSV (quoted above) seems to be saying, perhaps, that the Kingdom of God is operative among people now—not just in some future heaven. Or maybe Luke is saying that in Jesus, the Kingdom of God was, even then, with the people. But, there might be a better way to understand this.

In researching the wording of this passage, 60 translations were reviewed. About half of those translated the word "among" as "within." The Kingdom of God is within us. In this reading, Jesus seems to be saying that the Kingdom of God is in people's hearts. I really like the way that the Phillips translation puts it. In that translation, we read that the Kngdom of God is "inside" of folks.

This brings us back to the idea of listening, pressing on to know God, and solitude and prayer. Perhaps, part of our journey is not just outside of ourselves but learning to make connection with the Spirit already given to us in baptism.

John 14:8–9—Philip said to him, "Lord, show us the Father, and we will be satisfied." Jesus said to him, "Have I been with you all this time, Philip, and you still do not know me? Whoever has seen me has seen the Father.

Here, Philip really gets at the heart of the mystic's search. The mystic wants to see God; to know God intimately; to have an experience of God. Jesus tells Philip how to reach that place where God is known. Know Jesus. Pure and simple, to know Jesus and truly see Jesus is to know and see God.

Exodus 33:11—Thus the Lord used to speak to Moses face to face, as one speaks to a friend.

This is really what it is all about, isn't it? To be a friend of God? One thing that sets friendship apart from other relationships is mutuality. There is a back and forth, a give and take to friendship. There is two-way communication. There is a need for each other. When folks are friends, they learn from each other. When folks are friends, sometimes all they have to do is quietly sit in each other's presence. Friends tell each other secrets. That is what friendship is all about.

MYSTICS IN THE CHURCH

There have certainly been many in the church over the years who could easily claim the title of mystic. In the Hebrew Scriptures, Isaiah wrote about seeing the Lord: *"I saw the Lord sitting on a throne, high and lofty; and the hem of his robe filled the temple,"* (Isaiah 6:1). Seeing the Lord was no less an experience of the mystics in the New Testament church. Paul wrote of being caught up to the "third heaven" and having visions of God (see 2 Corinthians 12). Of course, the book of Revelation is filled with visions, auditions, and mystical experience.

In Catholic theology, there is a term, "the beatific vision," that refers to the direct experience of God that is enjoyed by those in heaven. This should be distinguished from the experience of God by those on the earth. Here, our experience of God is indirect, while in heaven it is immediate. Still, it must be said that in some measure, the Christian mystics seem to partake of something of the quality of the beatific vision while on earth. In fact, many claim to have had a direct encounter with God. The most well-known cases of a direct encounter with the resurrected Christ occurred with the conversion of St. Paul. Paul, then called Saul, was a persecutor of Christians. In his life changing encounter with Christ, he meets Jesus. As Acts 9 tells the story, Saul saw a great light and a voice spoke to him: *"Saul, Saul,"* the voice said. *"Why do you persecute me?"* He asked, *"Who are you, Lord?"* The reply came, *"I am Jesus . . ."*

The list of mystics in the church throughout the ages is a long one indeed. It reads like an honor roll for the Jesus Movement. But, we must never forget, as Olivier Clément has pointed out, mysticism was the main way that Christianity was understood throughout the patristic period. Many folks who had an experience of God were just regular folks—humble folks—not super saints. We can think of Brother Lawrence, who maintained a moment-by-moment conversation with God. He was not a theologian or priest, but a cook. There have been many regular folks who have sought an experience of God.

This raises a question. What about Evangelicals' experience of God? In many ways, they speak like the mystics—though many would strongly resist that title or notion. They speak of knowing Jesus as your personal savior, asking Jesus into your heart, and having a relationship with Jesus. Yet, it must be admitted that Evangelicals seem to have a different experience than Catholic, Orthodox, Anglican, and Mainline Protestant mystics. Traditionally, mysticism is often rooted in mystery and knowing God through what cannot be known of God. It is the fruit of silence and seeking.

Also, it cannot be denied that when it comes to social issues and such concerns as war and freedom, today's mystics (those who are not Evangelicals) tend to end up miles apart from their Evangelical friends. Sometimes it can almost make you wonder if they are connected to the same God. But, God is one. None of this is to say that many Evangelicals do not have a warm and close relationship with God. One can hardly doubt the deep piety of writers like A.W. Tozer or Oswald Chambers. We may never know why non-evangelical mystics and Evangelicals are so far apart. The best we can do is leave it for the Good Lord to sort out!

WHAT ABOUT YOU AND ME?

> *"Seek the Lord while he may be found, call upon him while he is near . . ."* Isaiah 55:6

> *"From one ancestor, he made all nations to inhabit the whole earth, and he allotted the times of their existence and the boundaries of the places where they would live, so that they would search for God and perhaps grope for him and find him—though indeed he is not far from each one of us. For 'In him we live and move and have our being . . .'"* Acts 17:26–28

The call to the mystical way is not just for saints, prophets, and apostles. It is for all people. We all can seek and find God for "*God is not far from us.*" As we have said, mystical experiences are in our human DNA. They are waiting to be discovered. God is waiting to be discovered. You are invited by Jesus on a journey to the heart of God. You are invited to a journey to your own heart, where the Holy Spirit dwells. It involves resolve and effort, but it is mostly a pleasant effort and mostly involves learning to see in a new way.

When you read of the great saints throughout the ages, or hear of modern day spiritual giants and their experiences of God, resist the temptation to compare. We are all unique. Ephesians 2:10 states that *"We are what he has made us."* The word that phrase is translating is the Greek word *poema.* It is the same word that forms the root of the English word *poetry.* The writer is saying that we are God's poetry; we are God's artful creation. We are each unique. God wants to relate to us all in a unique way that will heal our souls. So, don't compare! "Press on" to know the Lord.

The mystical journey is not some hidden, secret path. It may be secret, but it is a secret hidden in plain sight. This journey is for all who are willing to take it. In the Seals and Crofts song,

We May Never Pass this Way Again, we read of how we must cast away our fears and sail our ships out on the open sea to make the journey of life.

We must gather our courage to make a journey that will likely reveal not only the good and righteous in our hearts, but also the broken and dysfunctional. But, we can make this journey because, no matter how broken we are, Jesus offers healing. When we see God, we are made whole.

This journey will take three things. First it will take time. You won't arrive in a day. But, if you don't start on the journey, you will never arrive. And, just to start means that you have already arrived part way there.

Second, the journey will take love. If you don't love God, you will never succeed in reaching the destination. If you do love God (which I assume you do!), get ready to learn to love God even more.

Finally, the journey will take grace. Grace works through faith. Yet, grace also creates faith. Grace is God's unearned, unmerited good will towards us. You cannot qualify for it. It just is. Grace makes us confident that as we reach for God, God also reaches for us. In fact, God reaches out to us first.

So, trust in the Lord! Walk with God! And get ready for the journey of your life!

SOME THINGS TO THINK ABOUT

1. Do you think of mysticism as something esoteric or ungraspable or as something that is a natural part of the human experience?

2. Have you ever had an experience that you might call mystical? Have you ever felt caught-up in an experience of the beauty of nature or the wonder of love? Have you ever had a time when you felt a special closeness to God? What are the most memorable parts of the experience? Do you find it hard to put into words?

3. What do you think most gets in the way of people and their search for God?

FURTHER READING

Clément, Olivier. *The Roots of Christian Mysticism.* Hyde Park: New City Press, 1993.

McColman, Carl. *The Big Book of Christian Mysticism.* Newburyport: Hampton Roads, 2010.

Jones, Rufus. *Studies in Mystical Religion.* London: Forgotten Books, 2012.

2

Mysticism and the Nature of God

I WANT TO OFFER a bit of a disclaimer about this chapter. As I planned this book, I envisioned something that would be practical and relatable. This chapter is probably the most complicated one in the entire book. I think it's important (obviously, or I wouldn't have written it). Some readers may find it a bit heavy. If you do, feel free to skip it—but I think the rest of the book will be more meaningful if you don't.

Mysticism, in all its forms, is all about having a direct experience of reality. In less theistic formulations, mysticism, by whatever name it is called, endeavors to experience the present moment in its fullness. Explanation and commentary are not looked to as the method of grasping reality, for the mystics desire an experience beyond what is easily explained. For these mystics, the goal is to fully grasp reality in all of its dimensions. Sometimes, this is achieved via meditation. This meditation usually focuses on one-pointed concentration which often involves the use of a mantra, or perhaps the breath. It can also involve concentrating on the body as one scans the body from head to toe, noting each sensation that is going on at a given time. I am always amazed at how much is going on in my body when I do a body scan meditation. I discover tension and stress. As I experience this, often I will experience a calmness and letting go. In this quietness, we can experience a certain enlightenment that is beyond words. Indeed, it was as he quietly meditated that the Buddha experienced a grasp of things that led folks then and now to call him the enlightened or awakened one.

For Christians and other theists, the ultimate reality is God. In this conception of reality, God is the creator and lover of the world. Believers in God have always had a yearning to know God directly. Abraham and Sarah, called friends of God, had a knowledge of the Ultimate, Moses, who talked to God face-to-face as a person talks with their friend, had a very real experience of God. Paul had his visions in which he encountered the Living Christ. The hunger for an experience of God is deeply implanted in the Judeo-Christian experience. Of course, we have the prime example of meeting with God in the Life of Jesus. The Gospel records many experiences of Jesus that have traditionally been associated with mystics and mysticism.

But, to really be drawn into this great cloud of witnesses, there must be some notion of who God is. In one sense, that is something no one but Jesus can really claim. One thing all the mystics seem to know is that God and the nature of God can never be fully known in this life. God always remains hidden, at least partially. The question is "Who is God?"

The Bible answers this question to an extent for Christians. However, many faith traditions have gone beyond just revealing statements in the Bible. Folks from these traditions have maintained that God, the creator, gave us minds and rational thought and we should use them. Many early church Mothers and Fathers were well versed in the thought of Aristotle and Plato and used that framework to understand scripture, and ultimately the nature of God. This very much came to full-bloom in the middle ages— the time of Aquinas and Bonaventure and Scotus. These and many other Christians at that time wrote elaborate and learned volumes about God and God's nature. Sometimes they wrote about the mystical nature of the knowledge of God (especially Bonaventure). A certain "understanding" of things was created and expanded on over the centuries. From this understanding, a picture of God as conceived in Christianity began to emerge. That consensus still dominates the understanding of God (and in fact, even in the other Abrahamic Faiths) to this day.

CLASSIC THEISM

This consensus about the nature of God is sometimes referred to as *classic theism*. There are many facets to the picture of God that emerges from classic theism. Here we are only going to concern ourselves with the attributes that have traditionally thought to offer a "big picture" view of God.

One aspect of the consensus that emerged claimed that God is all knowing. God knows everything. God knows what is going to happen tomorrow. God know every aspect of life in the world. By extension it might be said that God also controls everything. If God knows all, and God's knowledge is perfect, and God always knows what is going to happen, then whatever happens is already a done deal. Not only is God's foreknowledge perfect, but even the smallest details of everyone's life is known and ordained to be what it is. This idea seems to be expressed in Psalms 139:

> "O Lord, you have searched me and known me.
> You know when I sit down and when I rise up;
> you discern my thoughts from far away.
> You search out my path and my lying down,
> and are acquainted with all my ways.
> Even before a word is on my tongue,
> O Lord, you know it completely.
> You hem me in, behind and before,
> and lay your hand upon me.
> Such knowledge is too wonderful for me;
> it is so high that I cannot attain it." Psalms 139:1–6

There is a problem with this, however. Although many folks take comfort in knowing that God has marked out a future path for their lives, other people get stuck right there. If God knows something terrible is going to happen, why doesn't God intervene?

Does God deal with folks in a real, open-ended relational way, or is everything already decided? Are we all just actors in a production of which God is the director?

This problem is compounded by another one of the attributes of God, according to classic theism. God is all powerful. God can do whatever God wants. No one can resist God's will. This seems to be what St. Paul claims for God when he discusses how God "hardened Pharaoh's heart" at the time of the Exodus to oppose freeing the slaves:

> *"So, it depends not on human will or exertion, but on God who shows mercy. For the scripture says to Pharaoh, "I have raised you up for the very purpose of showing my power in you, so that my name may be proclaimed in all the earth." So then he has mercy on whomever he chooses, and he hardens the heart of whomever he chooses"*
> Romans 9:16–18

From this perspective, Pharaoh had no ultimate say in the matter. God had a master plan to demonstrate God's power which involved causing Pharaoh to resist God.

This has caused many Christians over the years to be conflicted. It has caused others to give up on faith. Bart Ehrman is a well-known scholar of religion at a major university. He was once an Evangelical Christian. Now, he is an agnostic. He was overcome with doubt about it all when he thought about God's problem. All power + all knowledge leads to the perennial question: God knows bad things happen, sometimes even very bad things. God is all powerful. So why doesn't God intervene for good instead?

Two more attributes of God are that God is all good and that God is perfect love. There certainly is a long history in Christianity of seeing God in that light. The mystics have especially tended to see God in that light. Julian of Norwich speaks of God's motherly love. She experiences God as the lover of her soul. St. Francis sees God as love. For Francis, when Christians love others they are following the example of Christ.

It's beautiful to have a picture of God as the greatest lover in the universe. Still, for folks like Ehrman, it only muddies the waters even more. God knows the outcome of everything. God perhaps even ordains them. God has the power to bring about whatever God desires. When one looks objectively at the world, that may be hard to take that at face value. Add to that God's ultimate goodness and perfect love, and it becomes a very fractured picture. If God is perfect love, God wouldn't have wished for the events to have occurred. If God is all good, God wouldn't wish for children to suffer and die from cancer. Yet, God knows, and God either ordains or permits it.

It isn't discussed in such terms today, but there is one more attribute of God that we need to mention to round out the picture of God in classic theism. God is unmoved. God is *impassible*. By definition this means that God is unable to feel pain or suffer. God, in this view, is moved by God's own intention, foreknowledge, and will, and not by emotion or empathy. It is difficult to take much comfort in that!

ANOTHER WAY TO SEE THINGS

There is another way to see the attributes of God. It is inspired by the philosopher Alfred North Whitehead. He taught philosophy at Harvard in the first half of the twentieth century. Whitehead's thought was about the nature of reality, including the nature of God. For Whitehead, the universe is relational. It is quite real, with at least some degree of randomness. The future can never be predicted, because all of the actors are free agents. All inhabitants in the universe affect each other. In this view, the universe is a bit like a freewheeling jazz band. Every player contributes to the whole, but in many ways, they are "making it up as they go along."

After Whitehead, many process theologians extended Whitehead's thought to apply more directly to the nature of God, and how God can be understood in real terms. While process thought agrees that God knows everything that there is to know, it is not held that God absolutely knows the future. Since God is a real being who knows the rules of the universe, God also plays by those rules. God cannot know the future absolutely because the future does not exist and is contingent on many actors and happenings. To the old question, "Can God make a square circle?" or "Can God make a stone too heavy for God to lift?", the classic answer is that God cannot do something logically impossible. Instead of absolutely *knowing* the future, God is like a real being, God has *intentions and plans* for the future. Process theology agrees that God is all loving and good. Because of that God's plans for the universe and all it contains are good and loving. But, because the future hasn't happened yet, God doesn't know how those plans will play out.

When it comes to impassibility and being all powerful, process thought claims a situation that is quite contrary to what classic theism claims. Here, God is seen throughout the scripture trying to implement God's good plans. Sometimes God succeeds, sometimes God's plans are frustrated. We see God's heart breaking over the disobedience of Israel. We see Jesus longing to gather people as a hen gathers her chicks under the protection of her wings. We see Jesus lamenting that he could not (Matt. 23:37). Impassibility is denied flat out. God is seen as intimately involved with people and feeling their pain, as when God in Christ was moved again and again with sorrow and compassion for the poor and dispossessed. The bottom line is that process thought says that we can't have it both ways. One question this raises is if God is all-powerful and all-knowing, yet not all good and all loving? That must be addressed because logical consistency demands we ask it. Or, just maybe, God is all good and all loving but God's and power must be understood in a qualified sense. God cannot be logically inconsistent.

WHAT DOES IT ALL MEAN?

I have found that I understand and relate to God much better from the vantage point of process thought than classic theism. God is a real God and really interacts with creation. God cares deeply about me and is touched by my problems and suffering. God works to further God's plan (God's good and loving plan) for my life, but God's power is one of drawing and luring me to what is best. God's controlling attribute is not power or knowledge but love. It is the characteristic of love to persuade and not to coerce; to convince, but not to compel. God is patient. That is why the evolution of human life took millennia and many false starts. God works with divine influence to achieve what is best for the world, but God's essential nature does not allow for God to be a despotic potentate. God always longs for the best for all God's creatures. Sometimes God's plans are frustrated. Perhaps this is what the Hebrew scriptures refer to when God states a course of action God will follow, but things don't turn out that way. Sometimes the phrase is used that "God repented" or relented of what God intended. This is especially the cases related to God's judgment (see for example Amos 7:6 or Jonah 10:3). When God's good plans don't work out, God will find another way. God's power works in concert with God's loving nature, and love does not compel (at least rarely and never totally). That is why we engage in petitionary prayer. We believe that it really does make a difference. In some "mystical" way, when we pray we become collaborators with God to heal the universe. Things don't always turn out as God might like. But, because of the nature of love and the nature of the universe, I do believe that love will win.

So, in our search for God, our relationship becomes that of a friend to a friend. We work in real concert with God. God is deeply involved with our lives and truly wants the best for us. That is why we seek God, that we might become as God is. And, God is, and always will be, perfect love. All of this matters because our beliefs and expectations about God affect our search for God. They can even color our view of the kind of God we find on our search. If God is just having us play a role in a play where all the parts are written, a true relationship is impossible. If God relates to us in a real way, and open way, a give and take way, then, indeed, it is about becoming friends with God.

SOME THINGS TO THINK ABOUT

1. If there is a randomness in the universe, how can it be said that Love will win out in the end?

2. Why might the "perennial problem" drive some Christians away from God? How have Christians dealt with the problem in the past? How have you understood the problem?

3. Why do you think the notion that God is all loving and all good, but all knowing and all powerful in a qualified sense is shocking to some Christians?

4. Does it really matter how we view God's basic nature?

FURTHER READING

Ehrman, Bart. *God's Problem: How the Bible Fails to Answer Our Most Important Question-Why We Suffer.* San Francisco: HarperOne, 2008.

Mesle, C.R. *Process-Relational Philosophy: An Introduction to Alfred North Whitehead.* West Conshohocken Templeton Press, 2008.

Mesle, C.R. *Process Theology: A Basic Introduction.* St. Louis: Chalice Press, 1993

3

Mysticism and Poverty

"Blessed are the poor in spirit, for theirs is the kingdom of heaven . . ."

—MATTHEW 5:3

"Blessed are you who are poor, for yours is the kingdom of God."

—LUKE 6:20

THERE IS ONE THING that has always jumped off the page for me when I read the mystics. I certainly haven't read them all, but the mystics I have read seem to have something in common when it comes to using the Bible. They pay special attention to the Sermon on the Mount (Matthew) and the Sermon on the Plain (Luke). Take for example St. Francis. You have got to admit that he takes the Sermon pretty literally. In modern times, Dorothy Day, who founded the Catholic Worker Movement definitely was trying to live it out. Richard Rohr even wrote a book about it.

Why is it so important to them? I think it is because Jesus is so central to their expression of Christianity. Mystics seem to be radical disciples. The word *radical* is related to the word *root*. At its heart mysticism is not about having cool experiences. It is about seeking Jesus to follow him. Jesus is the root and tree; we are the branches. The Sermon has many implications for those who seek social justice in our unjust world. The mystics have always held that the goal of knowing God is perfect love. Love for God and love for neighbor. That's why it is important.

The words Jesus spoke in both presentations of the Sermon begin with the poor being blessed. The word that Jesus uses for poor is a word that just doesn't mean working poor. It means destitute. The poor are those that have nothing. They are worse off than the sharecroppers who are the stars of the show in so many of Jesus's parables. They are his listeners.

Of course, the rich are as well. Oh! It says "poor in spirit." Maybe he wasn't referring to literal poverty? Yet, Luke says nothing about the poverty being spiritual. Richard Rohr believes that the community that Luke was writing to was one of poor folks who could definitely relate to the idea of being poor materially. Matthew, in contrast was writing to a community trying to find acceptance in society. Rohr believes that these folks tended to be "better off" than Luke's community was, so he spiritualized Jesus' words. Maybe that's all wrong, though. A good public speaker might give her speech more than once. In fact, a good talk might be given many times. Maybe Luke and Matthew are recording events that took place in different places and at different times. Somebody is going to be blessed because of their poverty. Poor in spirit? Poor? Both? Which one is it?

Perhaps it is not terribly important whether Jesus is referring to material poverty or an attitude. In either case, they are *blessed*. That is an interesting word to use. The Greek word translated *blessed* is *makarios*. A better translation might be *happy*, or maybe even *happier*. Why are the poor happy? Because they are going to receive, or maybe they are right now receiving, the Kingdom of God. Someone might think joining a church might make them happy, or maybe praying. Nope, those things might make someone happy, but in this sermon, Jesus says that the poor are happy. Jesus' Kingdom that they receive—the Kingdom that makes them happy—isn't about food, or clothes, or stuff. It is about justice, peace, and joy (see Romans 14:17). It has wacky rules, where everything is stood on its head.

WHAT DO THE MYSTICS SAY ABOUT POVERTY?

Jesus was the mystic example for us all. In the story of Mary and Martha, we can see two very different reactions to a visit from Jesus:

> "Now as they went on their way, he entered a certain village, where a woman named Martha welcomed him into her home. She had a sister named Mary, who sat at the Lord's feet and listened to what he was saying. But Martha was distracted by her many tasks; so she came to him and asked, "Lord, do you not care that my sister has left me to do all the work by myself? Tell her then to help me." But the Lord answered her, "Martha, Martha, you are worried and distracted by many things; there is need of only one thing. Mary has chosen the better part, which will not be taken away from her." Luke 10:38–42.

Mary and Martha had two very different reactions to having Jesus in their home. Martha was a servant. She was working hard to serve Jesus because she loved him. Mary, on the other hand, was basking in the joy of Jesus' presence. Jesus certainly was not going to turn her away. We all need to sit at his feet and pour out our love as well.

But, can you imagine a world where people sit around just praying all day? Who would do the dishes? Who would fix the meals? Who would walk the dog? Who would take the kids to ball practice? If you prayed all day as you did your daily tasks, that would be one thing. But, in this story, Mary is sitting at Jesus' feet adoring him.

I think we need both. Francis was very clear that the friars shouldn't be cloistered monks. They were to work among the people. And the early Franciscans were definitely a mystical crowd. So, maybe the takeaway is that it is a good thing to love Jesus in your heart and soul, but also with your feet and hands. As Christians, we are called to work and pray. Perhaps we can put a spiritual spin on being poor. Still, there is something to be said for real poverty. The mystics have very often embraced actual poverty. Francis even gave away the clothes on his back. One of the premiere modern day theologians in the Catholic church is Karl Rahner. He wrote that the Christian of the future would be a mystic; one that bases his life on an experience of God, or they will "cease to be anything at all." So here we are, aspiring mystics, living the life of Mary and Martha. Will we work, or will we pray? We will be poor, or will we be poor in spirit? Or will we be both?

Dorothy Day took an incarnational approach to folks she encountered. In 1932, she was sent by Commonweal magazine to cover a hunger march in Washington. She went to church and began to pray that she could use her talents for the benefit of the poor. She saw Christ in everyone. For her, the doctrine of the mystical body of Christ impacted issues of racial justice, workers' rights, and issues of poverty and wealth. She lived simply and worked with the poor. And, she even went beyond working with the poor. In some measure, although her family of origin was not poor, she became poor in solidarity with the poor. She attended Mass daily, read scripture regularly, and studied the writings of the mystics of the church. She was a mystic who certainly believed that she was called to Christ-like poverty (remember that Jesus was poor).

We can also think of Thomas Merton. He had an encounter with Love while on a city street in Louisville. In his mystical experience, he had a deep sense of oneness with everyone in the world. He wrote later that he needed to embrace God in the whole world. He was a monk under a vow of poverty. He was also a social activist. It seems that mystics have felt a call to work for the materially poor, and at least in some measure, become like them. That is certainly the case with St. Francis, who called Lady Poverty his bride.

BLESSED ARE THE POOR

Jesus talks a great deal about wealth. In fact, he seems to tie conversion about money and wealth to embracing the Kingdom of God. Jesus doesn't say that his followers can't own property. He does, however, condemn the love of money, especially greed. Jesus' concern is that his followers might live a life without worry and anxiety. Often when we own stuff, it ends up enslaving us. We can't let it go. Wealth is addicting. Jesus wants to free us from worry. When Francis was encouraged to allow the brothers to own property, he said that, if they own property, they would need weapons to protect their property. In a sense, for Francis, to be broke was to be free from anxiety and bondage to things and the world's system of greed and anxiety.

The main emphasis of Jesus's teaching is the reign or Kingdom of God. Donald Kraybill calls that Kingdom an upside-down Kingdom. The Kingdom of God stands the social structures of the world on their heads. The poor are rich. Those that make peace and turn the other cheek are children of God. Those that are lowly inherit the earth. Jesus is concerned about wealth because it draws our attention from the Kingdom of God and puts it on wealth. Jesus said you cannot serve God and mammon (Matthew 6:24). And what is mammon?

The word originally referred a middle eastern deity; Mammon was the god of wealth. It refers to money, and possession. Jesus encouraged his followers to give more attention to God and God's Kingdom than to serving the god of possession:

> *"Do not store up for yourselves treasures on earth, where moth and rust consume and where thieves break in and steal; but store up for yourselves treasures in heaven, where neither moth nor rust consumes and where thieves do not break in and steal. For where your treasure is, there your heart will be also."* Matthew 6:19-21

As everyday mystics, we understand that possessions are not the be all and end all of life. We all have needs. And there is certainly nothing wrong with having some nice things that you like.

But, when our lives consist of acquiring wealth and we are running the rat's race, wealth owns us. The solution to this dilemma is pretty straightforward. Jesus once told a rich man to sell everything and give to the poor (Mark 10:21). The text says that before Jesus called him to poverty, he "looked at him and loved him." He knew that the rich man was a slave to things; he wanted to set him free,

Those who are blessed are beggars who stand before God knowing that all they own, all their money, everything they are and that they have is held in trust for God. And God calls us to be attentive to the needs all around us and how we can meet them. The Christian life is not really about doctrines or theological speculations. Those things are fine, of course, as long as they help us find what really counts with God- doing justice, loving mercy and walking humbly with God (Micah 6:8).

I think it is possible that voluntary poverty just might cause a person to feel a greater dependency on God. Still, I don't think that abject poverty is something that God is calling most people to embrace. God's desire is to change slums into decent living spaces. God desires everyone to have enough food to eat. God wants everyone to have quality healthcare. My family was quite poor, and for awhile when I was growing up, while we waited for dad's Social Security disability to be approved, our family had to look to the state for help. That was about 1968, and state help didn't amount to much. I went to a doctor very few times when I was sick. We all had serious dental problems. We had a very poor diet. I don't think that is a good condition for anyone to be in. It's not about living without that matters so much. It is about giving to others and not being a slave to things.

BLESSED ARE THE POOR IN SPIRIT

Why, in Matthew's account of the Sermon, did Matthew write that Jesus began the beatitudes with "Blessed are the poor in spirit?" Why does it come first? It is because that is the foundation of all that follows. It is the beginning of the Kingdom of God in our lives. We must be spiritually poor to live in the Kingdom. We must put aside all pride and the claim to live our lives in our own way. To be poor is to be without wealth. To be poor in spirit means that we understand that God is our sustenance. We understand that God is the one who feeds us spiritually. We are poor because we recognize that we are empty and that only God can satisfy our hunger and thirst. We pray and meditate because we must. Only God can supply our deepest need.

The real truth is that becoming poor in spirit might just be more of a task than becoming materially poor. I imagine that most of us have been pretty broke before—at least once or twice. But it is much more difficult to be humble and needy (and Jesus says again and again in many ways that we are all needy). When we become humble, needy, empty, it will be much easier for us to give of our material goods. When we try to decrease that Jesus might increase (John 3:30), we really recognize that we aren't self-sufficient. We need God's help. We are not up to the task.

As Donald Kraybill points out, the term poor in biblical context has three meanings. It does mean actual physical poverty. That cannot be ignored. It isn't just the poor in spirit who are blessed; it is the poor. The second sense of the term refers to the oppressed. These are the captives, slaves (to many things), and the desperate. The third meaning refers to humility of spirit, being poor towards God. We are called to give to the poor. We are called to recognize our desperation. And, we are called to be humble and needy towards God.

Being poor in spirit means putting away pride and our inflated sense of self-reliance and self-assurance. Like the old hymn says, "Nothing in my hand I bring, simply to thy cross I cling." Without God, we can do nothing. It is said that God helps those who help themselves. The truth is that God helps those that realize that they cannot help themselves.

What does all of this poverty stuff have to do with mysticism, with a direct experience of God? Isaiah writes:

> "For thus says the high and lofty one
> who inhabits eternity, whose name is Holy:
> I dwell in the high and holy place,

and also with those who are contrite and humble in spirit,
to revive the spirit of the humble,
and to revive the heart of the contrite." Isaiah 57:15

When we are poor in spirit, when we are humble and contrite, God dwells with us. God refreshes us and revives us.

HAPPY ARE THE POOR?

The word blessed means happy. Jesus says that the poor, either materially poor or spiritually poor, are happy. How can this be? Are we really happy when we are humble and needy? When we give away our wealth? When we "live simply that others might simply live?" We look to Jesus as our example:

> "[W]ho, though he was in the form of God,
> did not regard equality with God
> as something to be exploited,
> *but emptied himself,*
> taking the form of a slave,
> being born in human likeness.
> *And being found in human form,*
> he humbled himself
> and became obedient to the point of death—
> *even death on a cross."* Philippians 2:6–8

We are happy because we are following the Master. We are happy because when we are poor in spirit, we are becoming *"partakers of the divine nature."* We are happy because we are not playing the world's power games. We are happy because we are like a child depending on his or her parent, trusting in Mom's love and care. When we embrace gospel poverty, we find riches that are beyond description. We find that we are not poor but have the treasures of the Kingdom. We find our true life when we leave our life behind. Our life is not filled with worry. We are happy because when we are poor, we are really rich.

SOME THINGS TO THINK ABOUT

1. What does it mean to be "poor in spirit?"

2. Does having poverty of spirit excuse us from having any concerns about materialism? Can one be poor in spirit and materially rich? How might poverty of spirit affect our view of wealth?

3. How does poverty relate to humility? Is there a connection?

4. How does poverty relate to our experience of God?

FURTHER READING

Kraybill, Donald. *The Upside-Down Kingdom, 5th ed.* Harrisonburg: Herald Press, 2011.

Rohr, Richard. *Jesus Plan for a New World*, Cincinnati: Franciscan Media, 1996.

Sider, Ronald. *Rich Christians in an Age of Hunger (reprint edition).* Nashville: Thomas Nelson, 2015.

4

Mysticism and Love

Jesus said, "'You shall love the Lord your God with all your heart, and with all your soul, and with all your mind.' This is the greatest and first commandment. And a second is like it: 'You shall love your neighbor as yourself.' On these two commandments hang all the law and the prophets."

—MATTHEW 22:37–40

"Love has been perfected among us in this: that we may have boldness on the day of judgment, because as he is, so are we in this world. There is no fear in love, but perfect love casts out fear; for fear has to do with punishment, and whoever fears has not reached perfection in love. We love because he first loved us."

—1 JOHN 4:17–19

YOU DON'T NEED TO read the Bible very long to begin to get the picture that love is a big deal. In fact, one writer says that the only goal we are aiming for when learning about the Christian faith is love (1 Timothy 1:5). It's all about love. Love for God. The love of God. Love for our neighbors. Even love for ourselves. In the 60s, the Beatles sang, "All you need is love. Love is all you need." I must say that Jesus is on the same page. He loved us and tells us to love each other in just the same way. *"Love one another as I have loved you,"* (John 13:34–35).

When you think about it, the world is desperately seeking love. Folks look for it in many places. They seek it in friendships. They seek it in family. They seek love in marriage and romance. Folks even seek love and acceptance on social media. I even know a few married couples where the partners met on an online dating website. Somehow though, it seems that no matter how many relationships we have, no matter how in love we are, no matter how many folks friend us on social media, for many of us, we still feel empty. Indeed, love is all we need. But, how do we go about finding love? Or maybe we need a completely different lover. Maybe asking where we find love is the wrong question. Maybe love finds us.

"God is love," and when we love we are becoming like God. We are becoming *"partakers of the divine nature."* The world needs love. As this is being written (2020), our nation is deeply fragmented. What would it be like if we could learn to love each other? What if we loved one another as God loves us? I dare say that the discourse in homes and with our neighbors would be very different than it is now. Our political discourse would change. We might not agree with each other about everything, but we would certainly be gentle with each other. Love could turn our world upside down.

And maybe even more pertinent, what if we knew the love of God? What if we even had a special love affair with God? We think of mystics, such as John of the Cross, and we are amazed by the love they experience when they have an encounter with God. John also writes of the tender love he has for Jesus. That kind of mutual love can transform us. Indeed, it can transform the world.

HESED IN THE HEBREW SCRIPTURES

Even a very cursory reading of the Bible shows the supremacy of love. Love is the essence of the Christian life. But language in the Bible regarding God's love doesn't begin in the New Testament. The Hebrew scriptures have a great deal to say about love as well. Key to the Hebrew idea of love is the idea of *hesed* (often written *chesed*). The word is often translated steadfast love or lovingkindness. It is central to understanding how God interacts with humanity.

Hesed operates horizontally, from person to person, as well as from above, from God to us. On a person to person level it refers to actions and attitudes of goodwill towards family members, friends, and dinner hosts towards their guests. It can also refer to overtures of goodwill from a ruler to his subjects. It is a relational word.

That same notion applies to God's *hesed* towards people. It is relational, familial. It implies mutuality. It reflects a give and take. God shows God's love to God's covenant people by the very act of making covenant with them. The people of Israel are God's people. In a sense, they are God's family. *Hesed* means that God is not just a God way up there. God comes near to us and befriends us. God speaks with us, and the words God speaks are words of love.

Nothing can take God's *hesed* away. Nothing. God shows God's faithfulness in extending God's covenant love to people who can in no way earn it:

> "For the mountains may depart
> and the hills be removed,
> but my steadfast love shall not depart from you,
> and my covenant of peace shall not be removed,
> says the Lord, who has compassion on you." Isaiah 54:10

God's steadfast love is a permanent fixture. Whatever happens, it will always be there. Rooted in covenant, God's love will never end.

And *hesed* isn't just good feelings or intentions. This love is backed up by action. God doesn't just care, God acts. God's action is on behalf of the ones he loves. It is there even when it is least expected. Even when the people were unfaithful to the covenant,

God still loved. God pursued God's covenant people and went with them into exile. God's heart broke at their suffering. God's love never fails.

> *"The steadfast love of the Lord never ceases,*
> his mercies never come to an end;
> *they are new every morning;*
> great is your faithfulness."* Lamentations 3:22–23

> *"For great is his steadfast love toward us,*
> *and the faithfulness of the Lord endures forever.*
> *Praise the Lord!"* Psalms 117:2

LOVE IN THE NEW TESTAMENT

In New Testament times, there were four words used in the Greek speaking world to express the idea of love. One of the words, *eros*, forms the root of the English word erotic. It refers to physical, sexual love. That is certainly a very important kind of love! Without it, we wouldn't be here! However, this word is not used in the New Testament.

The other three words are used. Each share some similarity with the others, but there are differences. The word *storge* mostly refers to familial love. It is love such as exists between parent and child or sisters and brothers. The word is not common in the New Testament. I think most of us can relate to this kind of love. The cords that hold siblings together are strong. My sister lives a long way away from where I live, and I don't see her very much. Still, I care for her, think about her, call her, and pray for her. I love her! She is in my thoughts every day. If she is sick or unhappy, my heart goes out to her. If I can help her in any way, I would do it.

A second New Testament love word is *philia*. This refers to love between friends. The word is used frequently in the New Testament. It is a love between those who share common bonds, purposes, and ideas. Even though it is not a familial love like *storge*, it can be deeper. The church father Tertullian wrote "These

Christians, see how they love one another." In writing this, he was contrasting the fellowship of Christians to the relations of other folks in society. Although we might say that that comparison was a bit harsh, still, through all of the persecutions, poverty, and trials, they indeed did love one another.

The third word translated love in the New Testament is *agape*. This is the word commonly used to refer to the love of Jesus and God for people. It is an unconditional love. It doesn't depend on the beauty or intelligence of the one who is loved. It is a selfless love. It is the love that God has for us and that we are called to have for other people.

Agape love is genuinely benevolent. It expresses joy in the object of its love. It is unconditional goodwill. *Agape* is closely related to grace. Grace is unmerited favor. The love of God is expressed in God's grace. God's love is totally gratuitous. It is always there for us even if we don't return God's love. God's love is stronger than *philia* or *storge*- it is totally without conditions. It is more benevolent. It takes more joy in the object of its love. It is unlike the covenants in the ancient world. Those covenants expressed goodwill by mutual agreement. *Agape* is always caring, even if the object of love wants nothing to do with the lover.

The entire Christian ethic is based on love. It is love from God to God's people and the love of God's children for one another.

> "I give you a new commandment, that you love one an-
> other. Just as I have loved you, you also should love one an-
> other. By this everyone will know that you are my disciples,
> if you have love for one another." John 13:34-35

Jesus wants his disciples to love one another, and in fact, even those who aren't fellow disciples are to be loved with Christ-like love. And, Jesus doesn't just mean some honey sweet, gooey love. No. He means the real thing. The kind of love that rolls up its sleeves and does the hard work of love.

LOVE YOUR NEIGHBOR AS YOURSELF

Jesus says that the greatest commandment is to love God. The second is like it, he says. We must love others. It has been said that if we cannot love brothers and sisters who we can see, we cannot really love God who we cannot see (1 John 4:20). Somehow, loving God is deeply bound up with loving our neighbors. When you think about it, Jesus actually illustrated the great commandments by telling us what it means to love others. In that context, we are told the parable of the Good Samaritan. In another passage in the New Testament, we are told that the entirety of the Ten Commandments is summed up in the notion of loving others (Romans 13:9).

We are to love our neighbors as ourselves. That means that we must value ourselves. This starts by knowing what love is and knowing that we are loved by God. If we really don't love ourselves, we will not only be unable to love others, we will find it difficult to receive love as well. When we love ourselves, we see ourselves as being of value. We see ourselves as being treasured by God. We know we are loved by God when we experience God for ourselves. After all, God is love. Perhaps we need to start by contemplating how much God loves us; that God in Christ gave all for us, for all of us. "God so loved *the world*." The door is open to everyone. God loves each of us.

We need to love our neighbor, too. It is part of being like Jesus. Loving others is *"partaking of the divine nature."* When we love others, we give them the benefit of the doubt. Not only do we not speak ill of them, we don't even think badly of them. We turn to God when we are not loving others and ask God to give us love for them.

What does it mean to love? Paul described the nature of love. His description stands true whether we are talking about human love or God's love.

> *"Love is patient; love is kind; love is not envious or boastful or arrogant or rude. It does not insist on its own way; it is not irritable or resentful; it does not rejoice in wrongdoing, but rejoices in the truth. It bears all things, believes all things, hopes all things, endures all things."*
> 1 Corinthians 13:4–7

When we are patient with each other's faults, when we don't think ourselves better than others, when we don't demand our way, when we are kind and gentle, when we stick with folks to the end, we are loving our neighbor. When we do those things, we are *"partaking of the divine nature"* because we are being like God, showing the kind of love that God has for us.

The real test of our faith is love. Do we love as God loves us? God doesn't hold grudges or act resentfully. Jesus told us to pray that we might be forgiven as we forgive (Matthew 6:12). We cannot experience the freedom and release that forgiveness gives to us if we resent others and hold others to account for the ways they have hurt and wronged us, or for the ways others bug us. As some translations have it, *"Love does not take into account a wrong suffered."*

LOVE GOD WITH YOUR WHOLE HEART

As mystics, we should be immersed in a love relationship with God. Jesus said the greatest commandment is to love God with all our being. To love God means to keep God's commandments (John 14:15). The beauty of it is that God's commandments are for our own good. *"For the love of God is this, that we obey his commandments. And his commandments are not burdensome . . ."* (1 John 5:3). The things God asks of us are asked in love. We respond by obedience in love. God's commandments are not a burden to us because we love God so much.

We show our love for God when we pray. We can pray throughout the day. We may not get on our knees, but we can send out "arrow prayers" to God and bring God into our decisions and the little things of our lives. We enjoy spending time with our friends and sharing the little things of our lives. Should not the same be true of our friendship with Jesus?

We show our love for God by doing good works. Good works can never save us. But, the epistle says that we were made for good works (Ephesians 2:4). We don't do good works to be redeemed, but out of gratitude to God that God has already redeemed us.

We show our love for God when we love others—especially the poor, dispossessed, and those deemed unlovable. This is especially true when we love our enemies. God loved us and loves us still even when we aren't loving God back. We honor God when we love the folks that are hardest to love.

Jesus left us here to be his hands to bind the wounds of the suffering. We are his feet to go to the broken and needy and not wait for them to come to us. We are his voice to speak words of comfort and love to those crushed by the realities of life. We are the only hands, feet and voice that he has in the world. When we become Christ to a broken, lonely, angry world, we show our love for God.

We also show our love for God by our gratitude. When we come to God, we need to come with praise and thanksgiving. We show our love for God by appreciating how God loves us.

MYSTICS AND THE LOVE OF GOD

If mysticism is really about knowing and loving God, how can we be lost in that love? How can we experience God's love and not just talk about it? Once, when St. Francis was praying, he just repeated again and again, "My God and my All," completely lost in the love of God.

One simple thing that I have found helpful in my search to experience the love of God is to take my cue from Francis. I sometimes look at my favorite image of Jesus and think of his love for me. I begin, like Francis, to quietly say in my mind, "My God and my all." I don't really do anything but rest in the love of God. You might give it a try.

> "Set me as a seal upon your heart,
> as a seal upon your arm;
> for love is strong as death,
> passion fierce as the grave.
> Its flashes are flashes of fire,
> a raging flame.

Many waters cannot quench love,
neither can floods drown it.
If one offered for love
all the wealth of one's house,
it would be utterly scorned."
Song of Solomon 8:6–7

SOME THINGS TO THINK ABOUT

1. Have you ever been selflessly loved by another? What was that relationship like? How did you feel about being loved that way?

2. When have you felt that you have most loved another? How did you show that love?

3. When have you experienced the love of God? How have you expressed your love for God?

FURTHER READING

Rohr, Richard. *Essential Teachings on Love.* Maryknoll: Orbis, 2018.

Underhill, Evelyn. *An Anthology of the Love of God*, Wilton: Morehouse-Barlow, 1976.

5

Mysticism and Joy

FOR MANY YEARS, I was a professor of educational psychology. Of all of the courses that I taught at the college, it was my favorite. One of the topics I covered was temperament. Developmental psychologists often talk about the nine dimensions of temperament. These are basic characteristics in children that can often be discerned in infancy. In some measure, we carry the temperament that we are born with into adulthood. For each characteristic, children vary across a range of intensity and quality. The list of temperaments includes such items as activity level (children can be low energy or high energy), regularity (does the child approach her tasks in a predictable, methodical way?), approach and withdrawal (the extent of the child's eager engagement with others and the ability to embrace novelty), and intensity (the degree to which children put energy into their responses).

Maybe one of the most notable temperament characteristics in the nine dimensions deals with mood. Some children (and adults, too!) have a generally positive mood. Others tend to be less upbeat. I certainly see this in myself. I have always tended to be rather melancholy. When I see the glass, it is often half empty for me. I come from a long line of doom and gloom thinkers. Of course, being melancholy doesn't mean that I am never happy.

What can be said is that my melancholy temperament has become the perspective from which I view much of life. Sometimes it serves me well. At other times, not so much. But, that is who I am.

The Bible says that the Fruit of the Spirit is joy (Galatians 5:22–23). St. Paul writes that the real nature of the Kingdom of God is righteousness, peace, and *joy* (Romans 14:17). This is true (no doubt) even for the melancholy. Joy is a wonderful thing. Maybe that is one reason why the poor are blessed (remember that word really means happy). When our lives are not consumed with possession, perhaps we have less worry about losing them.

Dan Harris wrote a wonderful book about how meditating can cause us to be 10% happier. I'll take it! Ten percent more joy in my life would be a welcome addition. In the *Happiness Trap*, Russ Harris demonstrates how denial and the constant struggle against the problems in our life steal our joy of living. By letting go of our struggles, by stopping our battles against the aspects of our lives that we don't like, we can find true happiness.

One of the most interesting books on happiness is *The How of Happiness*. There we read that up to 40% of our happiness level is within our power to change. According to the author, we are not victims of fate. By mindful living and the practice of intentional optimism, we can move our set point for happiness to a much higher level.

The dictionary definition of joy describes it as a state of happiness. The definition goes on to say that joy is an emotion, evoked by success, good fortune or wellbeing. Words associated with joy include blessedness, bliss, delight, gladness and rejoicing. The antonyms of joy are even more telling. These include misery, ill-being, sadness and unhappiness. No one wants to go there!

However we understand it, we all want joy. The good thing is that God wants us to have joy too!

THE JOY OF THE LORD IS OUR STRENGTH

> *". . . this day is holy to our Lord; and do not be grieved, for
> the joy of the Lord is your strength."* Nehemiah 8:10

Joy is a wonderful thing! When our lives are filled with joy, life becomes something that we embrace with eagerness. Robert Louis Stevenson, at life's end, said that "to miss joy is to miss everything." I often wonder, in my melancholy way, how much of life I have missed out on by not finding joy in my everyday doings. I've heard it said that most folks are about as happy as they want to be. That may be true, at least to some extent.

Sadly, there is another side to life as well. That side is filled with darkness, heaviness, and sorrow. And, those who are depressed need to get help before worse things happen. When someone is clinically depressed, it is time get help beyond pastoral care. It is just the responsible thing to do.

But, even for those who are not clinically depressed, life certainly has its downside. We will all feel sorrow and sadness in our lives. But, I think that the mystics (who clearly weren't immune to depression) would tell us that on the balance, our lives should be joyful.

Everything doesn't have to be going our way to find happiness. The beatitudes certainly tell us that! The joy that the mystics know is the joy of knowing God. It is the joy of having a connection to something larger than ourselves. If we cannot find joy in our life circumstances, maybe it is time to change them. That certainly is the answer at least some of the time. But, even in the best of circumstances, problems can arise. That is why we need something (Someone) bigger than ourselves to give us meaning and richness in our lives.

Meaning is important. It is hard to feel joyful if life has little meaning. One of the main sources of joy is helping others find joy. Khalil Gibran said, "There are those who give joy, and that joy is their reward." When I was working as a minister, I saw this again and again. Often folks who were down and discouraged were so focused on their problems that they loomed like insurmountable mountains in their minds. Often, they saw themselves as lonely and friendless. Yet, I observed that those, with or without heartaches, who served others found meaning. They also found friends. Sometimes, those were the very things that saw them through the rough times.

As Christians, we are called to share the Good News. The Good News is that Jesus loves everyone. It is that God has reconciled all of broken and hurting humanity to Godself. The Good News is that in Christ, God has become one with us; that God knows the sufferings of humanity, and desires to heal this broken world. Broken people really aren't interested in our creeds or organizations. They need to meet Someone who can give them meaning. We preach the gospel best by living lives filled with justice, peace, and joy (Romans 14:17).

JOY IN RELATIONSHIPS

We don't only share the Good News with those who don't really know much about it. As sisters and brothers in Christ, we constantly share and show the Good News of Christ's love to one another. The writer of 2 John expresses the joy one has in relationships with others.

> *"Although I have much to write to you, I would rather not use paper and ink; instead I hope to come to you and talk with you face to face, so that our joy may be complete."*
> 2 John 1:12

Here, John says that his joy would be complete when he meets with other believers in person. There is joy in fellowship. Mark Twain wrote that grief can operate by itself, but to know the full value of joy, it must be shared with another. I think we all really want to do this. I know that if something good happens to me, I want to go home and share it with my wife. In fact, if I am down, or just feeling so-so, a visit from a friend can perk me up. There is definitely something special about friends. We need them. How sad it is that we can go to church with some folks for years and scarcely know their names! Something is wrong here.

Actually, our joy increases when we spread it around. When we are filled with joy, it should cause us to want other folks to experience joy as well. Joy is not diminished by sharing it. It is enhanced. Perhaps the best way to bring joy to other people is by serving them. When we go out of our way to do a kind deed to someone, even if we don't know them, we create joy. Many times, we have opportunity to share random acts of kindness.

In the town where I live (like about everywhere these days), there are people who stand on the corner holding signs saying that they are hungry. In the past. sometimes I would stop and give them some money. I met other people that said that these folks are just lazy freeloaders looking for money to spend on drugs or alcohol. They did have a point. You really didn't know what they did with the money you gave them.

Then it hit me. "Love believes all things," or so the Good Book says. They said they were hungry. Jesus said to feed the hungry. So, I decided that if I conceivably could, I would no longer give money. I would give them lunch. I started going to a grocery store or convenience store when I saw someone begging, and buying them food. Then I took the food back to where they were standing on the street and gave it to them and talked with them a bit.

The blessing was mine, to be sure. But, often the folks receiving the food expressed honest gratitude. Of course, I don't know if any particular person was really hungry for food, or if they really wanted money for other reasons. I just know that they said they were hungry, and I am a follower of Jesus. I am now taking them at their word. If I get ripped off, so be it. True joy comes in serving others and forgetting self. Many a preacher has said the joy means Jesus, Others, and You—in that order. It is a rather trite phrase, but in essence, it is true.

JOY IN SUFFERING

Joy in suffering! Brother, you say, you must be out of your mind! Maybe. I think my wife might agree with that assessment in some ways! Still, both she and I have had our share of suffering. I clearly remember the first church I served as minister many years ago. It really fell apart on me. After a couple of years, I decided to leave. And I don't just mean leave that congregation. I mean leave the ministry for good. My confidence was really shaken. I was hurting and bitter. My wife watched me come apart. It was hard on both of us.

I'm definitely not saying that I was happy about my shortcomings. I did however take some stock of the situation and years later, worked as a minister (successfully) for another ten years. Through all of that time in my personal wilderness, I had to come to see that God was with me no matter what. I took what little joy I had in that. They say that time heals all wounds. I'm not sure about that. I do know that over the years in my wilderness, I began my search into the nature of Christian spiritualty, beginning my journey to really know God. I'm still on that journey, and there I find joy even in the tough times. The writer of the Epistle put it this way: *"Rejoice always, pray without ceasing, give thanks in all circumstances; for this is the will of God in Christ Jesus for you."* 1 Thessalonians 5:16–18

Be sure to notice that we aren't asked to be happy or thankful *about* all circumstances. That would be exceedingly difficult. Who could be thankful for a divorce, a failed romance, a broken dream, or death of someone held dear? No, I don't think that God sends those things our way. We don't thank God for those things. The passage says "give thanks *in* all circumstances." I don't think this means finding the silver lining to every dark cloud. It does mean thanking God for the strength to get through the tough times. We may not be able to cure our sorrows or anybody else's, but we can still take joy in the thought that God will not forsake us. That is what it means to have joy in all circumstances.

We may not always win our battles. Gandhi said that "Joy lies in the fight, in the suffering involved, not in the victory itself." Joy makes it possible for us to bring God's saving love to every situation. In the Shepherd Psalm (Psalms 23), God doesn't take the lamb away from hard situations. Maybe God can't. But, right in the presence of difficulties, God "sets up a table" and I think that God dines with God's little sheep.

WAYS TO INCREASE JOY

> *"Although you have not seen him, you love him; and even though you do not see him now, you believe in him and rejoice with an indescribable and glorious joy, for you are receiving the outcome of your faith, the salvation of your souls."* 1 Peter 1:8–9

> *"You show me the path of life. In your presence there is fullness of joy; in your right hand are pleasures forevermore."* Psalms 16:11

The mystics have discovered that true joy is found in knowing God. When we love Jesus, when we sit at his feet and pour out our love, we find our greatest joy. Jesus says that when we see him, we have a joy that no one can take from us (John 16:22). In listening to Jesus, our joy is made complete (John 15:11).

Joy is a Fruit of the Spirit (Galatian 5:22). As such, like all fruit, joy grows as a natural part of the tree. Yet, as a fruit farmer knows, orchards take a lot of work. Trees must be pruned from time to time. Sometimes new branches are grafted in. From the tree's perspective, I doubt if these would be pleasant activities! But fruit grows better because of it. So also with us. We are sometimes pruned by life, but if we know Jesus, if we listen to him, we will develop the fruit of joy.

As mystics, we find our joy in our relationship with God. The Psalmist says: *"In your presence there is fullness of joy"*, (Psalm 16:11). It would seem a reasonable conclusion that the more time we spend with Jesus, the more joyful we will be. Having a regular prayer time is essential to living a joyful life. One way to have such a regular time of prayer is to make use of the Daily Office. There are other forms of daily prayer as well. For those whot feel a bit daunted by the Office, there is *Daily Prayer*, published by Liturgical Training Publications. They publish an updated book issued each year. The important thing is to establish a regular practice.

As Dan Harris has written, meditation can add to your happiness. There are many forms of Christian meditation and some are detailed later in this book. It does take some work to meditate (of course, it might also be said that meditation is the antithesis of work). Many good guided meditation and relaxation programs are available for beginner meditators.

One practice that many happiness researchers have recommended is keeping a happiness journal. At the very least, we can write a few sentences about four or five good things that happen to us during the course of the day. Then we can give thanks to God for those blessings. There is certainly something to be said for counting our blessings. To live without gratitude is a great sin.

Another practice recommended by happiness researchers is writing a letter of gratitude to someone else. At the very least, we can tell someone else that we appreciate them and why we do. It will no doubt increase your joy. And the real beauty of it is that while you are increasing your own joy, you can increase the joy of another as well. It has been said that love isn't love until you give it away. The same could be said of joy.

SOME THINGS TO THINK ABOUT

1. When you think of joy, what synonyms come to mind? If joy was a color, what would that color be? If it had a texture, what would it feel like?

2. When are you most joyful?

3. Is church a joyful place for you? Why or why not? What could you do to make the worship of the church more joyful experience of worship for you?

4. What are some concrete steps you can take to find more joy in your life? In your experience of God?

FURTHER READING

Harris, Dan. *10% Happier (reprint edition)*. New York: Dey Street Books, 2019.

Harris, Russ. *The Happiness Trap*. Durban: Trumpeter, 2008.

Lyubomirsky, Sonja. *The How of Happiness*. New York: Penguin, 2007.

6

Mysticism and Peace

PEACE! IS THERE A more beautiful word? We can face almost anything if we have peace in our hearts. When we have inner peace, we are happier, healthier, and in a better frame of mind. And, when we are at peace with others, we are living the life of the gospel. Jesus tells us that the peacemakers are happy. They are the sons and daughters of God (Matthew 5:9). I really don't think that Jesus is referring to peace between people and nations alone. I think he also is referring to inner peace. Peace is a package deal. It is difficult to have peace in your heart when you hate others. It is difficult to have peace with others when you are fighting conflicts within.

Jesus gives us peace as a gift. He is very clear about this.

> "Peace I leave with you; my peace I give to you. I do not give to you as the world gives. Do not let your hearts be troubled, and do not let them be afraid." John 14:27

Note that the peace that Jesus gives is not just like everyday peace. That peace is situational. When everything is going our way, we are at peace. But, Jesus's peace is there within us no matter what the circumstances. At least that is goal of the mystic's journey. A peace that is real. A peace that endures. Isn't that the kind of peace we need?

Also, notice that in this passage we also see the antithesis of peace: troubled hearts and fear. Perhaps this gets at the two types of peace that Jesus calls us to seek. Peace within (when we do not have troubled hearts), and peace with others and in the world (when we don't live lives where we strike out at others because of fear). Wouldn't it be great to live in a world that was all about peace?

THE DRAFT (A LONG TIME AGO)

I was born in 1956. It really wasn't until my teenaged-years that I became aware of the draft. By that time, I had become a Christian. There were many young men in my church that were conscientious objectors who were completing government approved alternate service at a local hospital. Maybe that is what got me thinking about war and my response to it as a Christian. Maybe another contributing factor was that the war in Vietnam was dividing our country, and many were questioning that war and war in general. Another influence on my thinking came from my parents- especially my mom. My parents definitely had little use for war. My mom told me what a waste of life war was many times. However, I think the biggest contributor to my thoughts about war was the Sermon on the Mount.

When I was 17, young men could still be drafted. The draft ended in 1973. I was 17 in 1973, so I had to register. I really wasn't much of a news hound in those days (I am far too much now I fear!), so I wasn't really aware that soon the draft would be ending. I had read the Sermon on the Mount several times. Although I had just started my mystical journey then, and was years away from identifying it as such, it seemed to me that I couldn't serve in the military. I knew Christians that did, and I certainly didn't feel it was my place to judge them. It just seemed to me that, if I served, I would be violating my vow to Jesus that I would follow him, even if it got hard. That included loving all folks—even my enemies (Matthew 5:43–48). I did resolve not to judge, but, for me, military service didn't make sense.

So, when I went to the draft board office and registered, I told them that I was a conscientious objector. I had thought about it before I made my mandatory visit at the office to register. I didn't know what it all meant, but I knew, in some way, I was bucking the system. The woman who took my information told me not to worry, that the draft was ending and that I would never be called. Some friends thought I was courageous to go to the draft offices and tell them that I wouldn't serve: Really though, it wasn't a particularly brave act. The objectors who had to face a draft board, as well as possible jail time, are the brave ones. All that my action caused was perhaps a little indignation from the folks working at the draft board office. Still, to this day, I think I did the right thing.

PEACEMAKERS IN THE EARLY CHURCH

It has been pointed out already that the dominant paradigm for the Christian life in the patristic era is mysticism. Out of that mystic heart of Christianity emerges a very unified voice that declared Christians are called to a life of nonviolence and peace-making. A general rejection of violence was the predominant stance taken by the vast majority of Christians until the mid-fourth century. There have been many books published filled with quotes from early Christians displaying their commitment to peace and their refusal to participate in violence. Here are just a few examples . . .

> *"We who by our prayers destroy all demons which stir up wars, violate oaths, and disturb the peace are of more help to the emperors than those who seem to be doing the fighting."*
> Origen

> *"To those who ask us whence we have come or whom we have for a leader, we say that we have come in accordance with the counsels of Jesus to cut down our warlike and arrogant swords of argument into ploughshares, and we convert into sickles the spears we formerly used in fighting. For we no longer take 'sword against a nation,' nor do we learn 'any*

more to make war,' having become sons of peace for the sake of Jesus, who is our leader, instead of following the ancestral customs in which we were strangers to the covenants."
Origen

"Christians have changed their swords and their lances into instruments of peace, and they know not how to fight."
Irenaeus

"The Lord, in disarming Peter, disarmed every soldier."
Tertullian

"Peace and love require no arms. For it is not in war, but in peace, that we are trained." Clement of Alexandria

"I do not wish to be a king; I am not anxious to be rich; I decline military command . . . Die to the world, repudiating the madness that is in it." Tatian

"We who formerly used to murder one another now refrain from even making war upon our enemies." Justin Martyr

It would seem that the early Christian mystics (for as we have discovered, mysticism was the dominant view of the church) embraced a wisdom often rejected by the world. As Taitian proclaimed, the Christians had died "to *the world, repudiating the madness that is in it.*" To these early Fathers and Mothers, the violence the world so often followed was madness, they sought a new way; a different way. They felt the call to the way of peace. Is it just possible that, with mystical hearts, these Christians had experienced the love of the Risen Christ so deeply that they loved everyone? Like the mystic Thomas Merton when he had an experience of oneness and love towards all people while on a busy city street, had these mystical parents of our faith been transformed by the Spirit to take the less travelled road?

What does this mean for you and me? The way of the peacemaker often causes controversy. It's not always popular. Oftentimes, Christian peacemakers have been labeled unpatriotic. Sometimes they have been called cowards. Is it the path that all mystics must take? Here is where we must show our love for one another. When talking about deeply held positions where Christians differ, St. Paul gives some practical advice: We should welcome each other, *"but not for the purpose of quarreling over opinions."* Paul goes on to say, *"Why do you pass judgment on your brother or sister. Or you, why do you despise your brother or sister?"* Finally, about things about which Christians differ, Paul offers some useful advice: *"Let all be fully convinced in their own minds."* (Read Romans 14).

So how do we deal with this? First, we should not be judgmental. Second, we should each study the writings of the early Christians as they relate to violence and war. Those sources are easily obtained. Third, it would be beneficial to study the gospels and see what Jesus says about it all. And finally, and maybe most importantly, pray with an open mind that you might know what Christ would have you do. That is what really matters.

The following vow of nonviolence is from Pax Christi, a Catholic peace organization. Perhaps we should all consider taking this vow as best we understand its meaning for us:

Pax Christi Vow of Nonviolence

> Recognizing the violence in my own heart, yet trusting in the goodness and mercy of God, I vow to practice the nonviolence of Jesus who taught us in the Sermon on the Mount—*"Blessed are the peacemakers, for they will be called [sons and daughters] of God . . . You have heard that it was said, 'You shall love your neighbor and hate your enemy.' But I say to you, 'Love your enemies and pray for those who persecute you, so that you may be [sons and daughters] of your Father in heaven,'"* (Matt.5:9, 43-44).
> Before God the Creator I vow to carry out in my life the love and example of Jesus
>
> - by striving for peace within myself and seeking to be a peacemaker in my daily life

- by accepting suffering in the struggle for justice rather than inflicting it
- by refusing to retaliate in the face of provocation and violence
- by persevering in nonviolence of tongue and heart
- by living conscientiously and simply so that I do not deprive others of a means to live
- by actively resisting evil and working nonviolently to abolish war and the causes of war from my own heart and from the face of the earth.

God, I trust in your sustaining love and believe that just as you gave me the grace and desire to offer this, so you will also bestow grace to fulfill it. *Pax Christi USA*

GETTING ALONG WITH DIFFICULT FOLKS

Some folks just get under our skin. They bug us for reasons that we can't even put into words. Other folks—maybe the ones we work with or even live with—can be downright mean and spiteful. Some folks we just seem to have conflict with. We must be around them, but our personalities clash. Sometimes folks on the other side of our politics can really infuriate us. Now, we are not talking about issues of global conflict (although it is closely related on one level). We are talking about our lives as we live every day with our family, friends, co-workers, and neighbors. We are talking about folks like the rude person in the line at the grocery store. Regular happenings, regular stuff.

In some ways, it is much easier to take bold positions about war and gun violence than it is to get along with your boss Bob or your cousin Nancy. Being a pacifist (as by now you have likely guessed I am), can be a pretty cerebral thing. But, the day-to-day stuff is, in many ways, the real nitty-gritty. It is an important issue for us as mystics. If you have been to a monastery, somewhere where you expect to find a collection of mystics, you probably noticed that they are quiet places. That is by design. Quiet around us can contribute to quiet within us. And peace is a large component of quiet. So, what can we do to get along with folks that disturb our peace? Here are a few suggestions.

1. *Listen to them.* Sometimes folks just want to be heard. Sometimes they are difficult because they think no one cares about them. My wife was a special education teacher for many years. She often dealt with children with an attention deficit disorder. I have often thought about how that problem is named and wondered how many of those children's greatest deficit was that no one paid them much attention. People want to be noticed. Even adults. Even if they don't know it. People will often act in annoying ways when they really just want someone to listen to them—to notice them. We can always listen to folks, even annoying folks. And we can respond in ways that show we care.

2. *Don't be judgmental.* I once heard a story about a mother and daughter at an Evangelical church getting in the car in the parking lot after the service. The mother looked over at the car next to her and saw a man lighting a cigarette. She said to her daughter, "Look at that! Only 5 minutes out of church and already smoking!" The daughter replied, "Look at that! Only 5 minutes out of church and already judging!" Everyone deserves the benefit of the doubt. We need to examine ourselves every day and note our good points as well as our shortcomings. When we see how far we fall short of the mark, we will be more inclined to be merciful to others.

3. *Don't argue with others.* My mom always told me that the quickest way to lose all your friends is to talk about religion or politics. The longer I live, the more I think that Mom was a very wise woman. Often, we are sure that we are right and the other person is wrong. We need to remember that we don't have to fight the battle of rightness. Acceptance and Commitment Therapy often sees our problems like a tug-of-war match. We are pulling against someone with whom we can never win. But there is one thing we can do to solve our

dilemma. We can drop the rope. Just get out of the battle. Maybe you are right about things, maybe you aren't. But, when things get hot, drop the rope.

INNER PEACE

The gift of God to mystics is peace. That is what we find when we listen to Jesus:

> *"I have said this to you, so that in me you may have peace. In the world you face persecution. But take courage; I have conquered the world!"* John 16:33

The message of Jesus should bring us peace. That is why he spoke his words to us. It is a Fruit of his Spirit and part of our inheritance as citizens of the Kingdom of God. That peace that Jesus speaks of here is peace of heart. It is inner peace.

I'm glad that is Jesus gift to us because, by nature, I am not a very peaceful person. I come from a long line of anxious people. I need peace. I want peace. In many ways, peace is the fruit of meditation and prayer. When we come to Jesus in prayer, humbly asking him to heal us of all of our worry and anxiety, he hears our prayers. God can use many ways to help us when we are anxious about our lives. God has many ways to help us with our hurt and anger. God might use the counsel of a faithful spiritual director. We might find peace through confession of our shortcomings with a priest or minister. Or, God might use a mental health professional.

One thing that we can do to help us find inner peace is to focus our efforts on things that we can control. Some things we can fix, and somethings we can't. What we can't control, we need to turn over to God. One of the main tenants of AA is that alcoholic's lives are out of control, and that they need to turn over control of their lives to a higher power. The language of AA is such that this must be admitted by those in recovery. In many ways, all of our lives are out of control. When we turn our lives over to God, we begin to let go of the things that we cannot handle and trust that God will make a way for us.

We also need to learn to relax. When we feel stressed out, we can take some time to be quiet and do some deep breathing. This has long been demonstrated to help calm us down. It can be done anywhere and anytime (well almost). It has been shown to slow the heartbeat and calm the body's tensions. And, while you are practicing 5 minutes of deep breathing, you can end with a prayer, asking God for peace. Many folks find help in practicing yoga, which combines movement and breathing exercises.

One very useful thing we can do to find inner peace is to simplify our lives. This might mean downsizing. Living a simple life works because when we aren't being a slaves to buying and selling, we are less concerned about our possessions. Jesus said:

> *"Take care! Be on your guard against all kinds of greed; for one's life does not consist in the abundance of possessions."*
> Luke 12:15.

And that about says it all.

SOME THINGS TO THINK ABOUT

1. What are some practical steps you can take to be a peacemaker in the world? In your town? In your church? In your family?

2. What should a Christian's response be when they encounter other Christians with whom they disagree about important issues?

3. Why is it so hard to get along with some folks? Do you think other folks ever find you hard to get along with?

4. What are you going to do this week to find and maintain inner peace?

FURTHER READING

Whitmire, Catherine. *Practicing Peace*. Notre Dame: Sorin Books, 2007.

Wink. Walter. *Jesus and Nonviolence*, Minneapolis: Fortress, 2003.

————. *Peace is the Way*. Maryknoll, Orbis, 2000.

7

Mysticism, Prayer and Mediation

THE NEW TESTAMENT TELLS us to *pray without ceasing* (1 Thessalonians 5:16–18). James reminds us to pray for one another that our brokenness might be healed (James 5:16). Jesus was a man of prayer. Mystics desire to be like Jesus, so they are people of prayer. This life of prayer is reflected in the *Book of Common Prayer* by its inclusion of the Daily Office—Morning and Evening Prayer. Some folks find the Office dry and monotonous. That need not be the case. One can pray daily prayer using the New Zealand Prayer Book, The Church of England Daily Prayer Book, The Society of Saint Francis Prayer Book, or many other sources.. The benefit of using a form for prayer is that it adds structure. Sometimes when we begin our mystical journey—and even if we've been on the path a long time—we don't know where to begin with our prayers. The Daily Office gives us a way to set aside time for God, and offer that time as a gift to God. The nice thing is that the Episcopal Daily Office is available from many sources online (such as The Mission of St. Clare). It is a good place to "get your feet wet." The Daily Office is rich with many prayers going back centuries.

Brother Lawrence, in *Practicing the Presence of God*, describes how he prays without ceasing. For him, God was a very present reality. He would talk with God about his daily tasks as he performed them. He would offer quick, on the spot prayers as he made day by day decisions. For him, God was a friend, and he knew that friends like to chat. He was the cook at the monastery, not well known, and he was not a theologian. He was just a regular guy, like you and me, who loved God.

As mystics, sometimes we pray with words and thoughts for people and situations. Sometimes we pray in silence. In Psalm 46, the Psalmist writes, *"Be still and know that I am God."* There is so much noise in our lives. There is the noise of people, and noise of cell phones and technology all around us. We need time to get away from all of that noise and encounter God. We also seem to have an abundance of noise in our minds, as we get drawn into the cares and concerns of our daily living. How can we seek God with quiet hearts? Although there are no rules for how to pray, over the centuries Christians have discovered certain practices to be helpful. In various forms these have come down to us today.

CENTERING PRAYER AND CHRISTIAN MEDITATION

One practice that many disciples have found helpful in seeking God is the practice of Centering Prayer. Thomas Keating has provided simple guidelines for Centering Prayer. This type of prayer is not difficult to understand. The way to go about it is simple—although you must commit to stick with it, for it to "work." Usually folks will spend 10–20 minutes daily in Centering Prayer. Here are the guidelines:

1. Choose a sacred word as the symbol of your intention to consent to God's presence and action within.

2. Sitting comfortably and with eyes closed, settle briefly, and silently introduce the sacred word as the symbol of your consent to God's presence and action within.

3. When engaged with your thoughts, return ever-so-gently to the sacred word.

4. At the end of the prayer period, remain in silence with eyes closed for a couple of minutes. (Keating)

We choose a word that shows our desire and intention to focus on God. Centering Prayer folks often say that it is a prayer of intention, not necessarily attention. In my own life using the prayer, I have found that it is about attention as well. The use of the prayer word focuses my attention, as well as showing my intention to God.

The guidelines for Centering Prayer recommend spending a few minutes in quiet before beginning to ask the Holy Spirit for a prayer word. Some folks stick with that prayer word for years, other folks feel a call to change it from time to time. Whatever word you choose, do not change it during any given prayer session. Instead of using a word, you might focus on the breath if that is easier for you.

Although the guidelines state that the prayer word itself has no real intrinsic value, it is useful as a sign of your intent to be silent before God. I have found that the word does often have inherent meaning for me. I choose my word carefully. It is the word that best expresses my experience of God at that time. Sometimes, I might choose a word like "love." Other times, I might choose something along the lines of "freedom" or "let go."

When we do Centering Prayer, we need a relatively quiet place. You want to sit comfortably, but you don't want to be so comfortable that you go to sleep. Almost all types of mediation instruction include directions to keep the back straight. That just doesn't work for me. I have rheumatoid arthritis, and I do much better in a recliner. The important thing is to discover what works best for you. Generally, I close my eyes.

We begin by saying the prayer word or words slowly in our mind, focusing on them. We listen to them, but we don't want to think about the meaning so much that we are distracted by thought. When we arrive at a place of quiet, we stop repeating our prayer word and silently sit before the Lord, attentive to whatever God wants to give us. When thoughts arise, we return to saying our prayer word until we are inwardly quiet again. The quiet is more important than the mantra.

After you are done (and I recommend you use a timer—there are many mediation timers available as apps for your phone), it is important to thank God for your time together. It might be a good time to pray the Lord's Prayer.

Although Contemplative Outreach states that the minimum prayer time should be 20 minutes, I have found that folks—especially beginners—have a difficult time meditating for 20 minutes. If you can pray like this for twenty minutes, you should do so. But, if you can only pray for ten minutes (or even five), go for it. If your time becomes a real struggle with the clock, you will not like the practice and will likely give up on it.

It is recommended that you ignore any insights or mystical experiences that you have during prayer, as these are distractions. I think that we should seek God and not theological insights or supernatural experiences. But, I guess I disagree to an extent with this guideline. I think, that when we quiet our hearts before God, that may be the exact time that God reveals Godself to us. There are many examples in the lives of the saints where the course of their lives was changed by a vision or insight from God during prayer.

Another type of prayer was discovered by John Main. This type of prayer is rooted in Eastern mediation practices and the experience of the desert monks in the early centuries of the Church. The organization that is devoted to this practice is called the World Community for Christian Meditation. This is how WCCM describes the practice:

> Sit down. Sit still with your back straight. Close your eyes lightly. Then interiorly, silently begin to recite a single word—a prayer word or mantra. We recommend the ancient Christian prayer-word "Maranatha". Say it as four equal syllables. Breathe normally and give your full attention to the word . . . The essence of meditation is simplicity. Stay with the same word during the whole meditation and in each meditation day to day . . . (L)isten to the word, as you say it. Let go of all thoughts (even good thoughts) . . . returning to (your prayer word) as soon as you realize you have stopped saying or it or when your attention wanders. (WCCM)

So, what's the difference? One way to see it is Centering Prayer is more like Vipassana (Insight Meditation), and Christian Meditation is more like transcendental meditation. They are both methods for quieting the heart and mind. Christian Meditation does it largely through the constant repetition of the mantra. Centering prayer does it largely through attentive silence. Christian Meditation is more rooted in the Christian Desert Fathers and Mothers where constant repetition of the phrase, "God come to my assistance" is encouraged. Centering Prayer is more rooted in a 14th century Christian prayer "manual" entitled *The Cloud of Unknowing*.

Which type of prayer is best? I think it depends on the person. In fact, there have been periods in my life where I have needed one method or prayer and other times when I have needed the other style. It is best to try each one for a couple of weeks and see which one works best for you.

Both of these types of prayer seem simple, and they are. Yet, as you start to practice them, you will probably find that it is easier said than done. It takes a commitment to stick with it in prayer and to keep coming back to God. If our mind strays a hundred times in a prayer session, and you find you have to keep returning to your prayer word, just remember that there is great benefit in the act of returning to God a hundred times. Nobody's perfect.

USING BEADS TO PRAY

The use of beads in prayer and meditation has a long history. They have been used in Christian tradition for centuries. They have also been used in other faith traditions. *Malas* have been used in South Asian religions for over 2000 years. This string of 108 beads is used to keep count in meditation. It is used to focus concentration and awareness. Typically, it is used while saying a mantra, either silently or aloud.

Muslim prayer beads are used to say short prayers while reciting the names of God. They consist of 99 beads, one for each of God's names. They are used to structure the prayers and keep count. The 99 names are considered attributes of God and appear in the Qur'an. The use of beads while doing recitations of the names is an accepted practice in orthodox Islam.

Evidence indicates that Christians have made use of prayer beads or prayer ropes since at least the 5th century. Early practice appears to have emerged with the Desert Fathers and Mothers— early believers that withdrew from society and took up residence in the deserts of North Africa. It is well documented that the Desert Mothers and Fathers prayed in ways that utilized phrases of scripture as a mantra. It is also known that Christians used prayer beads and ropes in conjunction with the Lord's Prayer.

Gradually, the use of beads and knotted ropes became what is generally thought of as the Catholic rosary. The use of the Catholic rosary normally involves prayers to Mary that are mostly derived from the gospels. Usually, the prayer goes like this:

> Hail Mary, full of grace
> The Lord is with you
> Blessed are you among Women
> And blessed is the fruit of your womb, Jesus
> Holy Mary, Mother of God
> Pray for us sinners
> Now and at the hour of our death.

The prayer is divided in such a way that certain parts of the prayer go with various beads. As with almost all types of meditative prayer, there is rhythm and repetition. Sometimes the prayer includes reflection of various aspects of Jesus's and Mary's lives.

The Eastern Orthodox tradition makes use of knotted prayer ropes to say the Jesus prayer. The prayer, "Lord Jesus Christ, Son of the Father, have mercy on me a sinner," is either prayed once at every knot, or the prayer is divided so that the words fall over 2 or more knots. Usually, the prayer is also coordinated with one's breathing. As the prayer is said, it is said slowly and from the heart.

One type of prayer beads I often use are Anglican prayer beads. The use of these beads originated in the Episcopal Church in the latter part of the last century—so they are a modern innovation. In this loop of beads, there are thirty-three beads, corresponding to the years of Jesus earthly life. These are divided into

4 groups of 7 beads with the additional beads located elsewhere on the loop. The beads are used to involve the tactile sense in prayer and as a counting device. There are many different ways to pray with Anglican beads.

Whenever beads are used as an aid to our mystical journey, it is mainly to calm the mind and focus attention. Very often, prayers involve repetition, coordinated with the beads as well as the breath. Sometimes, prayer with beads is used with the contemplation of an icon of Christ, Mary, or the saints.

THE POINT OF IT ALL

The point of it all—Centering Prayer, Christian Meditation, and prayer beads—is to settle the mind and direct the attention to Jesus. In prayers such as these, we sit in quietness and come to see God as God is. God is the unknown. Yet, God is near. Sometimes meditative prayer will break your heart. Sometimes you will be filled with overwhelming joy. Sometimes, let's face it, you will be fidgety and bored. The point is that no matter what, we all press on to the prize of partaking in the divine nature.

> *The Lord is in his holy temple;*
> let all the earth keep silence before him!
> Habakkuk 2:20

AN EXAMPLE . . .

I can share a bit about my daily prayer life. I usually get up in the morning and head for the coffee! Then, I retire to a room by myself where I can't hear any of the noise in the house. That is when I pray Morning Prayer from one of the Anglican or Catholic prayer books. I also pray a short Franciscan "Office." During this prayer time, I pray for needs of friends, family, and myself. I pray for folks in my church. I pray for peace in the world. Often, I also do Midday Prayer from the prayer book at noon. That is a very short prayer time (maybe 10 minutes).

Sometime, usually after lunch, I go back to my quiet room and read and pray about what I read from the writings of the mystics in the church. After that, I move into a time of quiet mediation. Often, I will do Centering Prayer, although I have modified the guidelines a bit to suit my personality. I might also pray with an Anglican rosary. I might pray the traditional way (Hail Mary . . .). I might pray with other words. Sometimes I will look at my favorite icon of Jesus. Often, taking my cue from Francis, I might inwardly repeat, "My God and My All." There are no hard and fast "rules." The goal is simply to still my racing mind and listen to God in silence. I'm sure that I normally don't spend more than half an hour on reading of the mystics and meditation. I have spent time journaling before, and many folks recommend it. But, I really don't care that much for it, and I do it only rarely. None of us are the same, and we must find our own way in prayer. Guidelines for prayer and meditation can be very helpful, but when you get down to it, it's not about methods, it's about you and Jesus.

Everyone has his or her unique situation. You might feel that you haven't got enough time for all of that praying. You might be right. Although it is really impossible to make the mystic journey without devoting time to prayer, you certainly don't have to follow my practices. You might need to use a shorter version of Morning Prayer, such as the *Daily Prayer* book mentioned earlier. You could probably find at least ten minutes or so for the kinds of prayer practices mentioned above. Don't get down on yourself if you can't give as much time to prayer and meditation as has been described above. The important thing is to start somewhere and see where the Lord leads.

Jesus said to his disciples, *"Come away to a deserted place all by yourselves and rest a while."* (Mark 6:31). He still calls his disciples to come away with him to the quiet to find rest for our souls. The question for us is whether we will go to meet with him. We have many obligations and activities to do during our day. What we really need to do is make a daily appointment with the God of love.

SOME THINGS TO THINK ABOUT

1. Which practice could you see yourself engaging with more, Centering Prayer or Christian Meditation? Why?

2. Why is it so hard for us to be quiet and still? What practices for stilling the mind have you found helpful?

3. Do you find it difficult to spend time in daily prayer? Do you think using some type of prayer book might be helpful?

4. Have you ever prayed with beads? Why might beads be helpful to some people when they pray?

FURTHER READING

Finley, James. *Christian Meditation*. San Francisco: HarperOne, 2004.

Keating, Thomas, *The Method of Centering Prayer*, Contemplative Outreach, available at https://www.contemplativeoutreach. org/sites/default/files/private/method_cp_eng-2016–6_0.pdf.

McGinn, Bernard. *The Essential Writings of Christian Mysticism*. New York: The Modern Library, 2006.

Meadow, Mary Jo. *Christian Insight Meditation*. Somerville: Wisdom, 2007.

Mission of St. Clare, *The Daily Office*, available at https://www.missionstclare.com/english/.

Liturgy Training Publications. *Daily Prayer*. Chicago: Liturgy Training Publications, 2020. (New publication yearly)

Vincent, Kristen. *A Bead and a Prayer*. Nashville: Upper Room, 2013.

World Community for Christian Mediation, *What is Meditation?* available at https://www.wccm.org/content/what-meditation

8

Mysticism and the Bible

*"Your word is a lamp to my feet
and a light to my path."*

—PSALMS 119:105

WHEN I FIRST BECAME a Christian and worshipped and fellow-shipped with the Jesus People in the early 1970s, the Bible was very important to me. It still is! In those days, I believed that the Bible was absolutely true and without error in any way. I was told by my pastors that the Bible has all of the answers that I would ever need. I could trust that the Bible was absolutely true because the Bible said it was true.

The truth of the Bible for me in those days extended to science and cosmology. The history in the Bible was absolutely correct. The timelines were correct. Morally, the Bible was perfect. I believed it all, but I did have to fight off some inner doubts. At first I viewed the doubts as pesky annoyances. Later they unsettled my entire world.

My doubts first began to multiply when I started attending college. In my science courses, I studied about natural selection and evolution. I was greatly disturbed by this, because it made very good sense to me. In my history and anthropology studies, I discovered that the timelines in the Bible left a lot to be desired. And the notion of people living eight hundred or nine hundred years had to be dismissed out of hand. All of this really shook me up. Sometimes I went about in a fog. I felt as if the rug had been pulled out from under me. I began to lose faith in the Bible.

When I began seminary, I discovered a curious thing. My professors engaged in the critical study of the Bible, and yet, somehow, on some level, they deeply believed the Bible as well. Obviously, they knew something that I didn't. Slowly, I began to see that the Bible was not a book dictated from heaven. It was a book about relationships. The history and the cosmology of the Bible might be way off, but the record of how people related to God was very true. I was taught that I could explore the ways that ancient folks related to God and how they perceived that God related to them. In that, there were lessons for me.

I still study the Bible. But now I don't feel as if must put my rational thoughts on hold. I find studying the Bible to be enriching, enlightening, and at times even exciting. Study of the Bible has always been a part of the Christian tradition. That is true today whether one speaks of Catholic, Orthodox, Evangelical, or Mainline Protestant traditions.

There are several reasons why Christians should study the Bible:

- We study the Bible so that we might understand the character and nature of God as it has been understood throughout the ages. We can also see how folks' views of God have changed over the centuries.

- We can learn from our ancient faith ancestors how the quest for God changed their lives.

- We can learn what shape that quest has taken.

- We can see where our parents in the faith failed to live out the highest ideals of a faith journey—even when they thought they were doing the right things.

- When we study the Bible, we learn a great deal about how to live a radically changed life and what that really means.

- The most important reason we study the Bible is because that is the only way we can ever hope to get any information about the life of Jesus

When we study the Bible, it is often good to have some help. Commentaries can be helpful, as can Bible encyclopedias or dictionaries. One simply accessed tool that virtually anyone can use is a good study Bible. A good study Bible used by many people is the *Oxford Annotated Bible*. In that work, you will find comments from noted scholars, maps, textual notes, and so on. There are other good study Bibles as well.

So far, we have been dealing with a more cerebral study of the Biblical text. That is important, since that forms the foundation for very much of our faith and life. Still, there is another way to approach the Bible. It is a way much more pertinent to us as mystics.

LECTIO DIVINA

The mystical approach to scripture is not overwhelmingly concerned about the contradictions in the Bible or whether or not this account or that account in the Bible is absolutely true. Instead of an academic or scholarly approach to scripture, mystics tend take a more devotional approach to the Bible. In the writings of the mystics, one sees a great deal of references to the gospels and the Song of Solomon, for example. You would be hard pressed to find discussions of the chronology of the Exodus or if the Israelites really conquered this or that nation. It is not that our mystic forebears in the past didn't have a more literal view of the Bible. They did. They lived before the age of modern science and psychology. The point is that they treated the Bible more like a love letter than a history book. In fact, it has been suggested by some scholars that the entire notion of historical "objective" truth was not much of a concern to people prior to the Enlightenment. Perhaps it is not so much that the mystics rejected that style of reading and writing as much as it simple didn't occur to them.

The approach that the mystics across the centuries took to the Biblical text is known as Lectio Divina. The main use of the Bible in Lectio Divina is to grow a friendship with God in Christ. It is about knowing and experiencing the living Christ. It is a way of using scripture as a part of an actual conversation between Jesus and us. It is about an ever-growing relationship with the Risen Lord.

Contemplative Outreach has provided straightforward guidelines concerning the practice. Here are the instructions concerning how to go about Lectio Divina:

Guidelines for Lectio Divina

1. Read the Scripture passage for the first time. Listen with the "ear of your heart." What phrase, sentence or even one word stands out to you? Begin to repeat that phrase, sentence or one word over and over, allowing it to settle deeply in your heart. Simply return to the repetition of the phrase, sentence or one word, savoring it in your heart.

2. Reflect, relish the words. Let them resound in your heart. Let an attitude of quiet receptiveness permeate the prayer time. Be attentive to what speaks to your heart.

3. Respond spontaneously as you continue to listen to a phrase, sentence or word. A prayer of praise, thanksgiving or petition may arise. Offer that prayer, and then return to repeating the word in your heart.

4. Rest in God. Simply "be with" God's presence as you open yourself to a deeper hearing of the Word of God. (Contemplative Outreach)

The phrase "Lectio Divina" means divine reading. That is what we are trying to do. We are not engaging in an inductive or deductive study of scripture (although earlier study might inform the practice). We are going beyond "head knowledge" and moving into "heart knowledge." It is not so much about knowing "what" as it is about knowing "Who", the Person of Christ.

To me, not all parts of the Bible are of equal use for Lectio Divina. My primary source for encountering God in the Bible is the gospels. But, to each his own! One can hear God speaking from many passages in the Biblical text.

This isn't a race to see how much of the Bible you can read in a day, week, month or year. Usually a verse or two is all you need if you go about the practice prayerfully. Remember, in Lectio all you need to have an encounter with the Divine is a word. So, read slowly.

Lectio Divina practice doesn't guarantee that you will hear God's voice. Some sessions will be powerful and life changing. Some will just be a time to rest in God. We do what we can, but we leave the outcome up to the Holy Spirit.

USING IMAGINATION IN DEVOTIONAL RESPONSE TO SCRIPTURE

Another way that we have a meeting with the Risen Christ is through the use of the imagination that God has given to us. Once again this works especially well with the gospels, particularly Matthew, Mark, and Luke, because it relies heavily on the power of stories. Jesus told stories (parables), and we can certainly explore them with our imagination. We can also tune in to the doing, dying, and rising of Jesus' life.

Take for example the account of Jesus walking on the water. Did he really walk on water? Some folks believe that he did. Others think that is a story modified, told and retold, and then written to teach a lesson. Those questions might be important in constructing theology or exploring historical facts.

However, we are using scripture in a devotional, mystical way. There is a time and a place for studying this passage critically. But, for our purposes, we are more about spending time with our friend. The passage in question goes like this:

*"He made the disciples get into the boat and go on ahead
to the other side, while he dismissed the crowds. And after
he had dismissed the crowds, he went up the mountain by
himself to pray. When evening came, he was there alone,
but by this time the boat, battered by the waves, was far
from the land, for the wind was against them. And early in
the morning he came walking toward them on the sea. But
when the disciples saw him walking on the sea, they were
terrified, saying, 'It is a ghost!' And they cried out in fear.
But immediately Jesus spoke to them and said, 'Take heart,
it is I; do not be afraid.'"* Matthew 14:22–27*

To go about using our imagination to encounter Jesus, we
begin with a prayer asking the Holy Spirit to guide our thoughts,
open our hearts, and change us. We read the passage a couple of
times—and we read slowly. Then we put ourselves in the story.
Maybe we see ourselves as one of the disciples. We feel the spray of
water on our face. We see the waves. We let ourselves experience
the fear. We see a figure on the horizon. We note that he is actually
walking on the water! We feel the confusion and the fear that they
felt. What kind of fear was it? We explore the fear that we would
feel if we were in the boat. Then we recognize Jesus. What do we
feel then? We see our fellow disciples. Are they comforted now?
Are they doubtful? And how do we feel when he gets in the boat
with us? How do we see ourselves responding?

The point is to experience Christ as he is presented in the
gospels. Sometimes, in accounts such as this, you can put yourself
in the place of Jesus. What would he be feeling about it all? What
look is on his face? We can see from many different perspectives
in the stories in the gospels. We might be Peter. We might be Zac-
chaeus. We might even be Pilate. It is all about spending time with
Jesus, discovering who he is, seeing him in our mind's eye.

PRAY READING (THAT TAKES ME BACK!!)

Many years ago, when I was still with the Jesus People, I heard
a simple, unassuming older man preach a sermon about how he

"used" scripture. Although I have changed in many ways since my Evangelical days, what he taught me to do is something that I still do. This way of reading scripture is especially useful for the epistles. In this approach to the Bible, we read a passage of scripture and "pray our way through." The idea is not to support doctrines or creeds. With this we are listening to God speak to us and responding to what it seems God is telling us. Of course, we begin by asking the Holy Spirit to guide us. I'll show you how it works using the first few verses of Ephesians 1.

Text

1. *Paul, an apostle of Christ Jesus by the will of God, to the saints who are in Ephesus and are faithful in Christ Jesus:*

2. *Grace to you and peace from God our Father and the Lord Jesus Christ.*

3. *Blessed be the God and Father of our Lord Jesus Christ, who has blessed us in Christ with every spiritual blessing in the heavenly places.*

Prayers

Verse 1 prayer—Lord make me faithful today. Whatever I do this day, may it be your will and for your purpose. May I be faithful to you.

Verse 2 prayer—Lord, cause me to see your grace all around me. Please take away all of anxiety and grant me peace.

Verse 3 prayer—Jesus, thank you for the spiritual blessings you give me.

As you read verse by verse, you might take time to stop after each verse and spend a few minutes in quiet. What you are doing is having a conversation. You have asked the Spirit to guide you and help you hear the voice of Jesus in scripture. Remember you are not doing theology. You are talking with a friend. It is very practical and very down to earth.

ANOTHER WAY TO APPROACH SCRIPTURE

Another way we might make use of scripture (or other Christian prayers or writings) is inspired by Eknath Easwaran's book, *Passage Meditation*. This approach really "straddles the fence" a bit between use of the Bible and meditating. It involves memorizing a passage of scripture which will be your focal point for meditation. While in the process of memorization, it is good to reflect on the meaning of the passage. You could do that using any of the approaches to the devotional use of scripture mentioned in this chapter. Although you might eventually memorize longer passages of scripture, you might begin with something with which you are familiar or something that isn't too long. A good place for many folks to begin is with the 23rd Psalm:

> "*The Lord is my shepherd, I shall not want.*
> He makes me lie down in green pastures;
> *he leads me beside still waters;*
> he restores my soul.
> *He leads me in right paths*
> for his name's sake.
> *Even though I walk through the darkest valley,*
> I fear no evil;
> *for you are with me;*
> your rod and your staff—
> they comfort me.
> *You prepare a table before me*
> in the presence of my enemies;
> *you anoint my head with oil;*
> my cup overflows.
> *Surely goodness and mercy shall follow me*
> all the days of my life,
> *and I shall dwell in the house of the Lord*
> my whole life long."

Many people are most familiar with this passage as it is found in the King James Version. Any translation you are familiar with will work well. If you don't have the entire passage committed to memory, a portion of it will work nicely.

After you have read and "prayed through" the passage, you will be using the passage for meditating. This is done by closing the eyes and silently repeating the passage one word or phrase at a time. It might go something like this: "The Lord . . . is my shepherd . . . I shall . . . not want . . . He . . . makes me . . . lie down . . . in green pastures . . ." Synchronize the words with the breath. The practice is to continue in this way throughout the passage.

We think about the passage when we are memorizing it and reading it. When we are using it for meditation, we simply "listen" to the words without commentary. It is important to resist the temptation to begin an inner "discussion." This often goes like this: "The Lord is my shepherd . . ." "Huh . . . How is the Lord like a shepherd? Maybe I'm like a sheep . . . I wonder if sheep will come right behind the shepherd? I wonder if . . . ??"

All of these thoughts may be fine thoughts. However, the point is not to figure things out while you are using scripture in this way. The point is to hear it, and let it become a part of you. We concentrate on the passage slowly. Word-by-word; really hearing it. If we set our meditation timer for 15 minutes and we are doing passage meditation, it is perfectly fine to question and explore the passage in a more intellectual way when you are done meditating. Resist the temptation to offer other prayers while doing passage meditation as well. The meditation itself is your prayer.

ENCOUNTERING THE LIVING CHRIST

> *"Indeed, the word of God is living and active, sharper than any two-edged sword, piercing until it divides soul from spirit, joints from marrow; it is able to judge the thoughts and intentions of the heart."* Hebrews 4:12

The Bible is an incredible book. Indeed, as Christians we believe that it contains a message for us that is inspired by God. As the scripture says, it is a living word. Christ is the Living Word. In our mystic approach to scripture, we desire to do more than obtain facts. We don't want to create theology. We aren't interested in winning arguments about religion. We want to meet with Jesus. We want a conversation with our friend.

As we encounter the Living Word through Lectio Divina, prayer reading, and activating the imagination to seek him, and doing passage meditation, we discover that we are changed. We see the truth of soul and spirit. Our thoughts and intentions—the intentions of the heart—are illuminated by the light. We are changed. More and more, we become *"partakers of the divine nature."*

This is all true, and I have found it to be true in my life. There is however an essential caveat. None of this will happen apart from the Holy Spirit. We encounter Christ through the Bible when our understanding is enlightened by the Spirit. Everything that we do in contemplative prayer must begin by the gentle teaching and mighty rushing wind and fire of the Spirit. God's voice thunders in our ears, yet it is a still small voice, and we must be quiet and listen.

SOME THINGS TO THINK ABOUT

1. Why do Christians argue so much about the inspiration and authority of the Bible? Can middle ground be reached? Is there a way to rise above the disagreements and engage with the scriptures together?

2. Why might Lectio Divina and the other practices mentioned here be valuable in knowing God? Is it possible that encountering scripture in those ways might be as valuable as academic Bible study?

3. Can you think of any Bible passages you already know that speak to you that might be useful for passage meditation?

FURTHER READING

Contemplative Outreach, *Lectio Divina: Listening to the Word of God in Scripture,* available at: https://www.contemplativeoutreach.org/sites/default/files/private/lectiodivinabrochure_2018_0.pdf.

Easwaran, Eknath. *Passage Meditation.* Tomales: Nilgiri Press, 2016.

Pennington, Basil. *Lectio Divina.* Chestnut Ridge: Crossroad, 1998.

9

The Tale of Two People

Dickens wrote the *Tale of Two Cities*, which is considered one of the greatest novels of all time written in English. I must admit that I have begun the novel several times, but soon gave up. The size of the book seems daunting, and the language is somewhat arcane. I am determined to read the whole thing someday. But, not today. Not yet.

But, I do want to borrow from Dickens (well, sort of!) and recount the *Tale of Two People*. I know these people very well and feel pretty qualified to tell their stories. They are the stories of Irene (my wife) and James (yours truly). The stories intertwine as one might expect. Yet, the two stories are very different.

THE STORY OF IRENE

Irene came from a middle-class family and grew up in a small town in Missouri. She spent her early school years in a small-town school. Her mom was a home economics teacher and her dad owned a locker plant. She remembers her childhood as a happy event. She grew up in what became the United Methodist Church. She has happy memories of Sunday school, confirmation classes, vacation Bible school, Christmas Pageants, and children's choir.

When she was in junior high school (as it was called then) her family moved to a larger town where her dad worked at a large grocery store as a meat cutter. Her mom continued her work as a teacher. Irene was involved with the church youth group, many activities in high school, and later at the community college in her town. In all of her school work, she usually finished at the top of the class.

THE STORY OF JAMES

My story is very different than Irene's. I grew up in Chicago, and from my elementary years through my high school years, in Kansas City, Missouri. My dad was a maintenance worker, machinist, and general handyman at places he was employed. My mom was a waitress, often at some pretty swanky places, and after we moved to Kansas City she stayed home. I have no happy memories of my family's church going because we didn't go to church. Well . . . That's not quite right.

There was a lady in our neighborhood who was always quite concerned that the young rabble-rousers in the neighborhood were going to hell. She was a very "straight-laced" lady and was a member of a very, very fundamentalist church in Kansas City.

To save the souls of us youngsters, she started a neighborhood Bible Club. I can't remember how I started attending, but somewhere at about eight years old, I did. It was great fun! We sang songs, marched around, and did crafts. But, there was one part that I really didn't like. She would always preach a little sermon and tell her young charges that they were going to burn in hell forever if they didn't get saved. She would then give an altar call.

I had never thought much about God at all before Bible Club days. However, as part of Bible Club we would get prizes for memorizing scripture passages. I have always had a great memory for such things and could usually outdo everybody. In fact, in writing this book, I easily "retrieved from memory" scripture passages from way back in Bible Club days.

The more I learned at Bible Club the more terrified of God I became. I was terrified of going to hell. As I got older, I became more fearful and also confused. My fundamentalist mentors told me that God is love. Yet, it didn't seem that way. I couldn't admit to myself what I really thought. Part of me, especially as I entered my teen years, desperately wanted to know the God of the universe. To know the God who loves all. Yet, I also hated God. God seemed vindictive and hateful. It seemed that God was saying that God wanted our love. And, it seemed that God was saying, "You better love me or else!" In my early teens, I'd had all of this God that I could take. I walked away from my friends and my church and just said forget it.

BACK TO IRENE

Meanwhile, back in small-town Missouri, Irene was meeting some fellow Christians that seemed to have a closer "walk" with God than she did. On a Christian retreat, she began to seek a deeper experience of God. She found it, too! It deepened her involvement in her Methodist Church. She made many friends who had experienced renewal. She was happy.

JAMES AGAIN

I was not so happy back in Kansas City. I can best describe it as an emptiness and anger. Empty, because I very deeply yearned to know God. Angry, because I didn't really like the God that I was being offered. Then, my life was changed. I met the Jesus People. They majored much more on the love of God than the judgment of God (but still retained a belief in eternal damnation). Slowly, I began to think that God really was love—even if all my questions weren't answered. I put my thoughts about the God who sent folks to hell on the back burner. The more I prayed and quieted my heart, the more it seemed that God always was love and nothing but love.

IRENE AND JAMES

I went to Central Missouri State University to earn a degree in elementary education. At the Christian campus ministry house, I met Irene. She was the most selfless, kind, and beautiful girl I ever met. She was free spirited and seemed to bring peace wherever she went. We became best friends. Then, we fell in love. On our wedding day (44 years ago), I thought I was the luckiest man on earth. After we married we attended an Evangelical church. I don't think that Irene really counted on how much I felt that I needed God. My old struggles started again; How could a loving God consign folks to hell? I became confused. My experience of God seemed to stand in opposition to what much of what that church was teaching. The struggles were mine. Irene's quiet faith and gentle love for God saw her through all of this.

BACK TO JAMES

Eventually, Irene and I decided that I should attend seminary. I did. First, I attended a Mainline Protestant seminary in Kansas City. Then, I was licensed as a minister by our denomination and sent to work in Eastern Colorado. I still needed to finish seminary to be ordained. There were certainly no graduate schools of divinity on the high plains of Colorado. My district executive and I decided that I would complete my seminary work in Denver. For various reasons (I don't think the reader really wants twenty pages expanding those reasons), I attended St. Thomas Theological Seminary, a Roman Catholic seminary (the seminary has since been closed).

I had become a very dissatisfied seeker of God by then (yep, lots of ministers are searching for something beyond themselves). But, at that seminary, I discovered that second life changing experience that impacted me ever after. I discovered there has been a long history of God seekers in the Church. Sometimes they were on the fringes of the Church, but they were a part of it all anyway.

It is these folks that sought God through quiet, meditation, contemplative prayer, and seeking God though God is hidden. Yet, these women and men also found that God is near. So, I started this journey, this mystical journey. I've been at it, for many years. I have been trying to follow Jesus through more than a decade of ministry, and even more years as a college professor. Several years ago, my mystical search led me to the Episcopal Church, which has a rich tradition of spirituality.

YES, IRENE ONE MORE TIME

What about Irene all this time, you might ask? What about her? Well, Irene continued to bring peace everywhere she went. In churches where I served as minister, she was always recognized as the stabilizer in our marriage. She not only put up with my mystical search, she encouraged it.

But, for herself, she has never strayed from that warm faith of renewal that she found on the retreat when she was a young adult, before we met. I meditate she does not. I practice Lectio Divina, she doesn't. I am on a Franciscan journey, as part of my mystical journey, she is not.

She loves folks deeply. She serves from the heart. She is often asked to do things at church and has often served on the vestry and in other capacities. Her love for God is real and obvious. I go on 3 day silent retreats. She gardens. She is optimistic and happy. I'm still often melancholy. She sees the glass half full. And, she's okay with that.

BOTH OF US

The point is that we are very different people. She has told me many times how much she thinks my mystical journey has been a benefit to me—and how by that journey it has been a benefit to others. Her spirituality is not restless. It is natural. She enjoys spiritual retreats and has gone on many. I can't complain that she doesn't join me on my journey. You see, she *knows* God, and the most amazing thing is that she has always known and loved God.

Once on a spiritual retreat that I attended we were asked to write down the person on earth we admired the most. Many folks listed their minister, their teachers, or some well-known spiritual giant. On my paper, I wrote *Irene*. What other name could I write? In all the years had known her, I realized that she had the most natural spirituality of anyone I know.

I think that some aspects of the traditional spiritual journey involving poverty, love, peace, and joy can enrich anyone's life. Anyone can benefit from meditation or Lectio. But, *and here is the point of it all*, I know that all of this is not for everyone. Some folks are like Irene. For whatever reason—the way they were raised, temperament, both—whatever, they have a very natural walk with God. It's just a part of who they are.

Yet, there are others that *must* commit to the mystical journey. For whatever reason—the way they were raised, temperament, both, whatever—they find God on the mystical journey. It is a lot of work, some might say, but the prospect of the joy that lies ahead urges them on. Such folks find joy in the journey. On the journey, they discover that they have a companion in their travels. Their companion is Jesus. From that they find joy. No one knows how far anyone will go on the journey. But, maybe, just maybe, it is the journey that matters.

FOR EVERYBODY

The take away here is don't judge! It is easy when we are on the journey to look at folks through our mystical eyes of poverty, love, joy, and peace and see how others don't measure up. It is not our place to decide who really knows God and whose knowledge is lacking. I have many old Evangelical friends. As things have gone totally crazy in our nation's discourse, we are often miles apart. Yet, I know those folks. Because I used to worship with them, I know they love God.

It is up to God to show them what might be wrong in how they view the world. It is up to God to show me where I am off the mark. I used to view things a different way also before the journey.

We need to realize that we may need our thinking adjusted in various ways as well. Judging is a sign of pride. God is the judge. And God judges on everyone's behalf:

> *"Who are you to pass judgment on servants of another? It is before their own lord that they stand or fall. And they will be upheld, for the Lord is able to make them stand."*
> Romans 14:4

God's judgment for everyone is one of acquittal for wrongs done. It is a judgment of good. It is a judgment of freedom and liberty. It is a judgment of peace and acceptance. One thing I learned in my years of running from hell is that God sends no one to hell. We make our own hells, right here and right now, whenever we run from God's love. Whether we are fully committed to the mystical journey, working with some aspects of it, or finding our own way, we can be assured of heaven now and forever. The call is to know God. The call is to know love.

That about wraps this little book up. The journey is before you. It is the journey of a lifetime. Whatever you are looking for, I sincerely hope you find it. Jesus said if we seek we will find; if we knock the door will be open. The question for us is will we seek? Will we knock? It's up to us.

> *" When you search for me, you will find me; if you seek me with all your heart . . ."* Jeremiah 29:13

And, I still think Irene is the most beautiful girl I know! Peace and All Good!

FURTHER READING

Gulley, Philip and Mulholland. *If Grace is True: Why God Will Save Every Person.* San Francisco: HarperOne, 2010.

CPSIA information can be obtained
at www.ICGtesting.com
Printed in the USA
JSHW051220290421
14053JS00005B/9